Getting Started with PhantomJS

Harness the strength and capabilities of PhantomJS to interact with the web and perform website testing with a headless browser based on WebKit

Aries Beltran

Getting Started with PhantomJS

First published: November 2013

Production Reference: 1191113

Published by Packt Publishing Ltd.
Livery Place
35 Livery Street
Birmingham B3 2PB, UK.

ISBN 978-1-78216-422-7

www.packtpub.com

Cover Image by Abhishek Pandey (abhishek.pandey1210@gmail.com)

Credits

Author
Aries Beltran

Reviewers
Phil Sales

Stéphane Wirtel

Acquisition Editors
Owen Roberts

Martin Bell

Commissioning Editor
Sruthi Kutty

Technical Editors
Menza Mathew

Amit Shetty

Copy Editors
Sarang Chari

Tanvi Gaitonde

Insiya Morbiwala

Alfida Paiva

Lavina Pereira

Project Coordinator
Joel Goveya

Proofreader
Lauren Harkins

Indexer
Tejal Soni

Production Coordinator
Nitesh Thakur

Cover Work
Nitesh Thakur

About the Author

Aries Beltran is a software developer located in Manila, Philippines. He works as an architect and R&D developer for financial businesses using web and enterprise technologies. He is currently developing new tools to provide real-time insights. He is interested in playing around with cutting-edge HTML5 development and mobile visualization. When he isn't coding, he likes to take photos of his daughter, Tara, who is his favorite model.

I would like to thank my family, Cecille and Tara, for inspiring me always and giving me courage to aim higher. I would also like to thank Phil Sales for helping me in every aspect of this book. Lastly, I would like to thank all of the people that I work with at Packt Publishing, who are very supportive and understanding.

About the Reviewers

Phil Sales is a software development manager and has worked in this role for more than 10 years. He started and managed development and testing teams for various companies, mostly in the banking sector. Most of his projects have been web application oriented, with a Java/J2EE flavor. His latest endeavor involved starting up a Manila office for a UK-based software vendor, with development, testing, and support teams. Based in Manila, he has also worked on projects in the US, the UK, and Thailand.

Stéphane Wirtel has been one of the main developers of the OpenERP project for the past six years. He is also a consultant for the high availability of OpenERP and for the SaaS architecture of OpenERP. He has been an enthusiastic developer and user of Linux for the past 15 years and has been working on Python for 10 years. He likes to discover new technologies (LLVM, Erlang, Golang, and so on).

He is also a member of the Python Software Foundation and a former member of the Association for Computing Machinery and the GNOME Foundation.

I would like to thank my wife, Anne and my daughter, Margaux.

www.PacktPub.com

Support files, eBooks, discount offers and more

You might want to visit www.PacktPub.com for support files and downloads related to your book.

Did you know that Packt offers eBook versions of every book published, with PDF and ePub files available? You can upgrade to the eBook version at www.PacktPub.com and as a print book customer, you are entitled to a discount on the eBook copy. Get in touch with us at service@packtpub.com for more details.

At www.PacktPub.com, you can also read a collection of free technical articles, sign up for a range of free newsletters and receive exclusive discounts and offers on Packt books and eBooks.

http://PacktLib.PacktPub.com

Do you need instant solutions to your IT questions? PacktLib is Packt's online digital book library. Here, you can access, read and search across Packt's entire library of books.

Why Subscribe?

- Fully searchable across every book published by Packt
- Copy and paste, print and bookmark content
- On demand and accessible via web browser

Free Access for Packt account holders

If you have an account with Packt at www.PacktPub.com, you can use this to access PacktLib today and view nine entirely free books. Simply use your login credentials for immediate access.

Table of Contents

Preface

PhantomJS is a fully scriptable headless browser. When I started using it two years ago, I thought it was just another environment that can perform and evaluate JavaScript, but, as I explored its features, to my surprise, I found it to be an awesome technology. Most of the features that are discussed in this book come from the bits and pieces of the application that I have been using in my work to create a web monitoring and user-simulation type of service. PhantomJS is one of those technologies that can be integrated into any existing platform and can solve web development puzzles, ranging from page manipulation to user event simulation.

This book is a guide to help you not only ease your way into developing scripts in PhantomJS but it will also show you the cool features of this technology. In addition, it will also encourage you to be more creative and play with it as each chapter unfolds new capabilities. This book will help you get started.

What this book covers

Chapter 1, Getting Started, starts by introducing what PhantomJS is, how to get and install it, and then goes directly into creating your very first script.

Chapter 2, Manipulating Page Content, shows you how to directly interact with pages that we open in our headless browser.

Chapter 3, Handling Events and Callbacks, explores how to capture events that web pages generate for the browser and reacts accordingly. We will also simulate browser events that involve simulating the users' mouse and keyboard events.

Chapter 4, Capturing Errors, focuses on how to handle errors within PhantomJS and those that are generated by the pages.

Chapter 5, Grabbing Pages, plays with one cool feature of PhantomJS, that is, capturing screenshots programmatically.

Chapter 6, Accessing Location-based Services, focuses on using existing web-based and location-based services. Using PhantomJS as our headless browser, we will be capturing location data and creating examples that are useful.

Chapter 7, Working with Files, shows you how to work with files and understand how these are supported by PhantomJS using its own FileSystem API.

Chapter 8, Cookies, discusses how cookies are supported by PhantomJS. We will learn to create cookies and interact with the pages that need them.

Chapter 9, External JavaScript, addresses the subject of working with external JavaScripts and shows how we can create PhantomJS modules that can be re-used in every script.

Chapter 10, Testing with PhantomJS, focuses on the use of PhantomJS for testing. We will learn how to use Jasmine, create test scripts, and make them work using PhantomJS.

Chapter 11, Maximizing PhantomJS, goes over the different products that are written using PhantomJS and shows how we can go beyond what we've learned from the books to make our own applications.

What you need for this book

You will need a Windows, Mac OS, or a Linux-based environment where you can develop and work with the examples given in this book. You will definitely need PhantomJS binaries, which will be discussed in *Chapter 1, Getting Started*, where we will learn how to get and install them.

Who this book is for

This book is intended for those who are interested in developing cool scripts and having fun at the same time, using JavaScript and PhantomJS. If you are a complete novice in JavaScript, this is not the book for you. You should also have working knowledge of HTML and CSS, but you don't need to be an advanced user.

Conventions

In this book, you will find a number of styles of text that distinguish between different kinds of information. The following are some examples of these styles, and an explanation of their meaning.

Code words in text are shown as follows: "The onLoadStarted event will be triggered when PhantomJS starts loading the page based on the resources received."

A block of code is set as follows:

```
var system = require('system');
var url = system.args[1];

var page = require('webpage').create();
page.onLoadStarted = function () {
  console.log('Page Loading Started');
};

page.onLoadFinished = function () {
  console.log('Page Loaded');
  phantom.exit(0);
};

page.open(url);
```

When we wish to draw your attention to a particular part of a code block, the relevant lines or items are set in bold:

```
[default]
exten => s,1,Dial(Zap/1|30)
exten => s,2,Voicemail(u100)
exten => s,102,Voicemail(b100)
exten => i,1,Voicemail(s0)
```

Any command-line input or output is written as follows:

```
$ ./phantomjs pageload3.js http://www.google.com
Loading takes 6.751 seconds.
0.255 seconds : http://www.google.com/
0.379 seconds : http://www.google.com.ph/
0.213 seconds : http://ssl.gstatic.com/gb/images/b_8d5afc09.png
0.676 seconds : http://www.google.com.ph/images/srpr/logo1w.png
0.561 seconds : http://www.google.com.ph/images/srpr/nav_logo80.png
6.135 seconds : http://www.google.com.ph/xjs/_/js/hp/sb_he,pcc/rt=j/ver=_
aDh7zAWqI8.en_US./d=1/sv=1/rs=AItRSTOgg467Qcx4GftzMMz3ZDPd84lcog
```

New terms and **important words** are shown in bold. Words that you see on the screen, in menus or dialog boxes, for example, appear in the text like this: "Using a simple page open, handling these two events will give us two console prints: **Page Loading Started** which is displayed first, followed by **Page Loaded**."

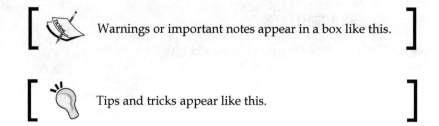

Warnings or important notes appear in a box like this.

Tips and tricks appear like this.

Reader feedback

Feedback from our readers is always welcome. Let us know what you think about this book—what you liked or may have disliked. Reader feedback is important for us to develop titles that you really get the most out of.

To send us general feedback, simply send an e-mail to feedback@packtpub.com, and mention the book title via the subject of your message.

If there is a topic that you have expertise in and you are interested in either writing or contributing to a book, see our author guide on www.packtpub.com/authors.

Customer support

Now that you are the proud owner of a Packt book, we have a number of things to help you to get the most from your purchase.

Downloading the example code

You can download the example code files for all Packt books you have purchased from your account at http://www.packtpub.com. If you purchased this book elsewhere, you can visit http://www.packtpub.com/support and register to have the files e-mailed directly to you.

Errata

Although we have taken every care to ensure the accuracy of our content, mistakes do happen. If you find a mistake in one of our books—maybe a mistake in the text or the code—we would be grateful if you would report this to us. By doing so, you can save other readers from frustration and help us improve subsequent versions of this book. If you find any errata, please report them by visiting `http://www.packtpub.com/submit-errata`, selecting your book, clicking on the **errata submission form** link, and entering the details of your errata. Once your errata are verified, your submission will be accepted and the errata will be uploaded on our website, or added to any list of existing errata, under the Errata section of that title. Any existing errata can be viewed by selecting your title from `http://www.packtpub.com/support`.

Piracy

Piracy of copyright material on the Internet is an ongoing problem across all media. At Packt, we take the protection of our copyright and licenses very seriously. If you come across any illegal copies of our works, in any form, on the Internet, please provide us with the location address or website name immediately so that we can pursue a remedy.

Please contact us at `copyright@packtpub.com` with a link to the suspected pirated material.

We appreciate your help in protecting our authors, and our ability to bring you valuable content.

Questions

You can contact us at `questions@packtpub.com` if you are having a problem with any aspect of the book, and we will do our best to address it.

1
Getting Started

PhantomJS is a new solution that provides headless testing of web applications. It is also a tool for dynamically capturing and rendering pages as images. It allows you to programmatically manipulate page content to control and change it to different forms. It can scrape websites and save important information to files. It will also provide you network-level information of your page and site resources. These are just a few of the functions that PhantomJS can do for us. It provides a fresh and a whole new way for web designers, testers, and developers to perform and create browser-based solutions.

PhantomJS uses QtWebKit as its core browser capability and uses the WebKit JavaScript engine for script interpretation and execution. Anything and everything that you can do in a WebKit-based browser (such as Chrome, Safari, and Opera browser) you can do with PhantomJS. It's more than just a browser because it supports web standards, such as CSS selector, DOM manipulation, JSON, HTML5 Canvas, and SVG; moreover, you can do some cool stuff such as performing file system I/O, accessing system environment variables, or even instantiating your own implementation of a web server daemon.

Downloading PhantomJS

Before we go through the features of PhantomJS, first we need to get our copy of the PhantomJS binaries. Typically, PhantomJS provides downloadable releases of binaries that are precompiled and packaged. You can choose from Linux, Mac OS X, and Windows precompiled packages. To download a copy, go to `http://www.phantomjs.org/download.html`.

Download your binaries based on your preference of operating system. After downloading, extract the binaries to any folder you desire. That's it! Your PhantomJS binary is ready to be used.

Add PhantomJS to PATH

Add the /bin folder of PhantomJS into your $PATH OS to make it easier when calling PhantomJS main binary. This allows us to call the binary anywhere without specifying the full path.

We will be using the Mac OS X version of PhantomJS throughout this book for running code examples. Don't worry if you are working on a different platform; the instructions are the same on all platforms.

Quick PhantomJS install on Mac OS X

As an alternative to downloading the precompiled binary, we can install PhantomJS using brew:

```
brew update && brew install phantomjs
```

For more information about brew, visit http://brew.sh/.

Building PhantomJS from source

You may also want to build your own binaries by compiling PhantomJS from source. Sources are hosted in the Github server at https://github.com/ariya/phantomjs.

Before you start downloading sources, you will need these tools installed on your workspace:

OS	Required development tools
Windows	Visual Studio 2010 or 2008 (Express edition)
	git
Mac OS X	Xcode
	git

OS	Required development tools
Ubuntu/ RHEL/ CentOS Linux	gcc
	gcc-c++
	make
	git
	openssl-devel
	freetype-devel
	fontconfig-devel

The PhantomJS team is always trying to find the optimal way to build the sources, and the build instructions are frequently modified. To build PhantomJS properly, you must follow the steps found here: http://phantomjs.org/build.html.

If you are not planning to hack into PhantomJS code and develop new features, then it is best to download the pre-packaged binaries.

Working with PhantomJS

Now, let's see how PhantomJS's magic works. It is a command-line-based application, so we need to execute it in an OS terminal or console. The PhantomJS package contains a series of files and comes with one main executable file, which is named phantomjs.

Open your terminal and then navigate to your PhantomJS bin folder. In the prompt, execute phantomjs without any arguments.

PhantomJS Windows build

In Windows build, PhantomJS executable can be found in the root folder with the filename phantomjs.exe.

Running PhantomJS without any arguments will give you an interactive prompt that is similar to the JavaScript debug console you could find in any modern browser. In this interactive prompt, we can execute JavaScript code line by line. This functionality is very useful for debugging or testing code before you actually build your script.

Say "Hello Ghost!" to PhantomJS using the interactive prompt. Using `console.log` will output any type of data to the output console of a JavaScript interpreter.

```
phantomjs> console.log("Hello Ghost!")
Hello Ghost!
undefined
phantomjs>
```

See? It is simple. Just like coding any JavaScript. But wait. What is that **undefined** message just after the **Hello Ghost!** message? That is not an error. It is just how the interactive mode behaves. Each call is expected to return data just like any ordinary function call and it also automatically outputs the data value to the output stream.

Since the `console.log` command does not return any value, the message is **undefined**. If we issue an assignment to a variable command, the following output will be displayed:

```
phantomjs> name = "Tara"
{}
phantomjs>
```

The assignment to a variable will take place and the result of the operation will be displayed. Because it is in the form of a string literal, the **undefined** message will not be displayed. The interactive mode is similar to a long-running script; any variable or function you define will be loaded into the memory buffer and can be accessed anytime during the session. So, based on our preceding example, the `name` variable can also be displayed by referencing it.

```
phantomjs> name = "Tara"
"Tara"
phantomjs> name
"Tara"
phantomjs> name + " and Cecil"
"Tara and Cecil"
phantomjs>
```

We can even use the variable with another operation as seen in the preceding lines of code. However, any operation's result that is not assigned to a variable will be available only during the execution of the line. The operation that concatenates the name variable with another string literal will be performed, and the resulting string will be displayed in the console but will not be kept in memory.

Objects can also be accessed within the interactive mode, and one of the most commonly used objects is `phantom`. Try typing `phantom` in the prompt and you will get the following output:

```
phantomjs> phantom
{
    "clearCookies": "[Function]",
    "deleteCookie": "[Function]",
    "addCookie": "[Function]",
    "injectJs": "[Function]",
    "debugExit": "[Function]",
    "exit": "[Function]",
    "cookies": [],
    "cookiesEnabled": true,
    "version": {
        "major": 1,
        "minor": 7,
        "patch": 0
    },
    "scriptName": "",
    "outputEncoding": "UTF-8",
    "libraryPath": "/Users/Aries/phantomjs/bin",
    "defaultPageSettings": {
        "XSSAuditingEnabled": false,
        "javascriptCanCloseWindows": true,
        "javascriptCanOpenWindows": true,
        "javascriptEnabled": true,
        "loadImages": true,
        "localToRemoteUrlAccessEnabled": false,
```

```
        "userAgent": "Mozilla/5.0 (Macintosh; Intel Mac OS X)
            AppleWebKit/534.34 (KHTML, like Gecko) PhantomJS/1.7.0
                Safari/534.34",

        "webSecurityEnabled": true
    },
    "args": []
}
phantomjs>
```

PhantomJS displays the content of the object when used in the interactive prompt, and even its own phantom object can be referenced. You may also observe that the object is displayed in the form of JSON and details every attribute of the object except for the function definition. Using this approach, we can also examine each and every object, and we will be able to know what the exposed attributes and available functions are.

Let's try using one of the most important functions available in the phantom object: the exit() function. This function will enable us to quit PhantomJS and return to the caller or to the underlying operating system.

```
phantomjs> phantom.exit()
$
```

This function signals the application to exit with a return code of zero or normal and without errors. Passing a numeric value as an argument of the exit() function denotes the error code to be passed back to the caller. This is helpful when trying to write scripts that need to verify if the execution was successful or if an error occurred and what type of error it was.

If we trap the error code in a shell script, it will look as follows:

```
#!/bin/bash
bin/phantomjs
OUT=$?
if [ $OUT -eq 0 ];then
    echo "Done."
else
    echo "Ooops! Failed.!"
fi
```

In the preceding lines of code, right after calling `phantomjs`, we capture the error code coming from the application using the `$?` function. We assign that to an OUT variable and then perform a test on it in the succeeding lines. If the error is equal to zero, then we display **Done**; otherwise, we say that the call failed.

```
$ ./trapme.sh
phantomjs> phantom.exit(0)
undefined
Done.
$ ./trapme.sh
phantomjs> phantom.exit(1)
undefined
Ooops! Failed.!
$
```

Use the interactive mode to experiment with the PhantomJS API.

Before we begin creating PhantomJS scripts, we first need to make a quick roundup of the PhantomJS JavaScript API.

PhantomJS JavaScript API

PhantomJS runs JavaScript and comes with a JavaScript API to make your life easy. It extends the standard JavaScript API and adds richer layers of capabilities, such as allowing us access to the underlying file system, ease of access and manipulation of DOM objects, system and environment variable gathering. It even gives us the ability to inject custom scripts into the web page.

But, be warned. PhantomJS is a very active community, and every now and then, changes are being introduced. New APIs and objects are being added, but of course, there are few items that are being changed, and ultimately some of them become deprecated or are totally removed. The PhantomJS website has a full list of all the functions and syntax, and has proper tagging for deprecated functions. We should visit it regularly to check for upcoming updates so that we can adjust appropriately in our codes.

The Module API

While writing custom objects and API sets, you may want to create custom modules that will make your life easier. You can do that in PhantomJS using the Module API. It allows you to create your own modules and import it anywhere in your implementation. The built-in modules are webpage, system, fs (File System), and webserver.

The WebPage API

PhantomJS is a headless browser. Accessing and manipulating web documents are its core functionalities, and that's what the WebPage API is used for. The WebPage API allows us to access, control, and manipulate web documents. It provides a rich interface to easily reference and extract page details including document content. It enables capturing of events, such as page loading, when an error occurs within the page, or when navigating to another page is requested, and so on. It is also capable of capturing pages and saving them as images. And more importantly, it allows you to manipulate documents on the fly and traverse DOM as you do with any web page. This is enormously valuable for writing automated user interface tests — for example, you can force click events or post forms, and capture the results — as well as standard web scraping of public URLs.

The System API

The System module provides system-level functionalities ranging from OS information, environment variables, command-line arguments, and process-related properties. The System module is very useful as you engage more in developing applications with PhantomJS.

The FileSystem API

Accessing files, writing to text files, or just reading a custom configuration file — these are tasks that can be done with PhantomJS. FileSystem provides a standard API to perform file I/O. You can read, write, and delete files; you can even list folder files.

FileSystem has 31 functions to manage and manipulate files within PhantomJS. We have been using this set extensively, and it helps solve several problems without fail. Writing JSON data to a file is very basic, but you will find it much easier using the FileSystem API.

The WebServer API

Perhaps you have a grand idea, but it requires you to process a web request and execute a PhantomJS script on it. PhantomJS can do that; you can embed your own web server implementation using the WebServer API within your PhantomJS application. This feature is marked as experimental, but it does work, and with roughly five lines of code you can have your own web server running.

This module is based on the open source Mongoose web server library that supports multiple platforms, authorization, web sockets, URL rewrite, and even "resumeable" downloads. For more information about Mongoose, visit `http://code.google.com/p/mongoose/`.

The phantom object

The `phantom` object is your reference to PhantomJS within your scripts that allows you to access certain properties and provides functionality that affects the entire script (such as quitting the application as previously mentioned.) The `phantom` object can be directly referenced anywhere in the script and does not need to be explicitly imported. You may also access it as a child of the global `window` object.

The `phantom` object allows access to relevant data, such as cookies and library paths. If we want to import or inject third-party JavaScript libraries, such as jQuery, we can do that using the `phantom` object. We can also create a "catch all" event handler for errors using the `onError` event of the `phantom` object.

PhantomJS not only allows us to harness the power of JavaScript but also gives us a very useful API. Each day, more and more contributors are enhancing this API, giving us more options and easier ways to solve real problems. We will learn more about these APIs as we continue our journey learning about PhantomJS.

The command-line arguments

There are a few command-line arguments that we need to understand before plunging into writing PhantomJS scripts. The syntax of the PhantomJS argument is:

```
phantomjs [switches] [options] [script] [argument [argument [...]]]
```

All of the arguments are optional. Using the command without arguments will bring up the interactive mode.

The script argument

The `script` argument is the name of a script file. It can be a relative or an absolute path and must follow the path convention of the host system OS.

```
phantomjs /scripts/chapter1.js
```

The script filename may or may not end with a `.js` extension. PhantomJS supports two types of scripting—JavaScript or CoffeeScript. We don't need to specify if the script is in JavaScript or CoffeeScript; PhantomJS will automatically detect it. We will be using JavaScript in our examples. If you want to learn more about CoffeeScript, you may visit the CoffeeScript website at `http://www.coffeescript.org`.

The debug option

The `debug` option enables the printing of additional warnings and the debug messages. This is very useful when debugging your script. It accepts either `yes` or `no` as the value of the option, and `no` is the default value.

```
phantomjs --debug=yes /scripts/chapter1.js
```

The cookie-file option

If you are working on pages that require persistent cookies, you need to enable this option. This option will accept a file path where cookies will be saved and read.

```
phantomjs --cookie-file=/scripts/cookies.txt /scripts/chapter1.js
```

Writing PhantomJS scripts

We know how to write JavaScript, and now we know that there are several PhantomJS JavaScript APIs and objects. We also have learned the basics of the PhantomJS command-line arguments. We are now ready to create our own scripts.

We will create a simple script to load a site and then display the title of the page when loaded successfully. Finally, we will exit. If the page fails to load, we will log some message to the console.

```
var page = require('webpage').create();
page.open("http://www.packtpub.com", function(status) {
    if ( status === "success" ) {
        console.log(page.title);
```

```
    } else {
        console.log("Page failed to load.");
    }
    phantom.exit(0);
});
```

The preceding PhantomJS script is very simple. First, we import the `webpage` module, create an instance of the `webpage` object, and assign it to a variable named `page`.

The `page` variable now holds an instance of the `webpage` module where an `open` function is available. Next, we instructed PhantomJS through the `webpage` instance to open and load the URL. The second parameter of the `open` function is a function callback definition that will be executed upon completion of the opening of the URL. Inside the definition, we check if the status is "`success`", and if it is, the page is loaded, and then we will display the title of the page. Then, we call the `exit` function to terminate the script. Let's save this code snippet as `helloweb.js` and execute it by passing the filename as our first argument to the `phantomjs` binary.

```
sources — bash — 120×14
$ phantomjs helloweb.js
Home | Packt Publishing

$
```

Summary

At this point, we have learned quite a few basics of PhantomJS, but this is just the tip of the coolness of the technology. We now know how to get started with PhantomJS, and create small scripts to play around with it. We won't stop here. We will now move on to the more interesting stuff that it can offer, such as manipulating web pages, simulating user events, and grabbing screenshots. So, let's do more PhantomJS coding in the succeeding chapters.

2
Manipulating Page Content

PhantomJS is a browser, and the basic function of a browser is to access web pages. In this chapter, we will learn various techniques of loading web pages in PhantomJS, and we will explore beyond using it simply as a headless browser.

Opening a web page

In a normal browser, opening a web page means typing a URL and letting the browser render the document fetched. It works almost the same way in PhantomJS, except that we don't actually wait for the page to be rendered before our eyes. Everything is done in a non-visual way. We don't see text, high-resolution images, or even animation on the page. We don't see anything that will show up on the screen.

We also do not type the URL in the address bar as we do in a normal browser. We create scripts to load the page. We learned in the previous chapter that to access a URL or a page in PhantomJS, we need to use the WebPage API.

```
var page = require('webpage').create();
page.open("http://www.packtpub.com", function(status) {
  if ( status === "success" ) {
    console.log("Page is loaded.");
    phantom.exit(0);
  }
});
```

And that's how we open a page in PhantomJS. So what now? We don't use PhantomJS just to browse a page, but for more useful tasks such as filtering search results from the Google search engine, extracting Twitter messages and saving them to a file, or performing assertions on objects and text content of the web page for testing and site verification. These are some of the useful features of PhantomJS, and we can do a lot more with it.

Let's try a simple example first, then we will move to a more complex one. We will open a page and display the title of a URL passed as the first argument.

```
var system = require('system');
var url = system.args[1];
```

We use the `system` module to retrieve the arguments. The first argument will always be your script filename, which will be at index 0 of the system arguments. The succeeding arguments are our script arguments, these can be of any use; for our example, we will assume that the second argument is a URL, as shown in the following screenshot:

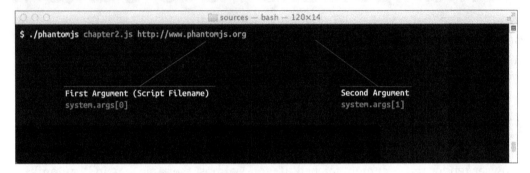

We will now use that variable to open the page.

```
var system = require('system');
var url = system.args[1];
var page = require('webpage').create();
page.open(url, function(status) {
  if ( status === "success" ) {
    console.log("Page is loaded.");
    phantom.exit(0);
  }
});
```

In the preceding code, we passed the `url` variable as the first parameter of the `open` function of the WebPage API. Now, instead of the message that displays when the page is loaded, we are going to change that to display the title of the page.

```
page.open(url, function(status) {
  if ( status === "success" ) {
    var title = page.evaluate(function () {
      return document.title;
    });
    console.log(title);
    phantom.exit(0);
  }
```

The document or page title can be retrieved from the DOM objects, and to access that in PhantomJS we need to perform code evaluation since it is within the context of the web page. We wrapped our code reference into the web page `evaluate()` function. Within the context of the page, we can access the `document` object, and using the DOM API functions and attributes, we extract the title of the page.

Basically, we cannot access DOM objects outside the `evaluate()` function context. The web page `evaluate()` function will execute our code on a different context, think that we are having another sandbox within PhantomJS. All of the code evaluated will only exist on that certain block and won't affect or allow us to modify other code outside of it.

With this, we cannot even return the DOM nodes that we manipulate within `evaluate()` and perform further processing outside of it. We should do all necessary parsing, retrieval of data from DOM, and the manipulation and changing of node values within `evaluate()`. If we want to return anything outside of the context, it is either with a simple type of data (such as a String), or we should wrap it as JSON-serializable data.

```
var system = require('system');
var url = system.args[1];
var page = require('webpage').create();
page.open(url, function(status) {
  if ( status === 'success' ) {
    var data = page.evaluate(function () {
      return {
        title: document.title,
        numberOfNodes: document.getElementsByTagName('*').length,
        documentUrl: document.URL
      };
    });
    console.log('Page Stats');
    console.log('-----------------------------
                      ----------------------');
    console.log('Title           : ' + data.title);
    console.log('URL             : ' + data.documentUrl);
    console.log('Number of Nodes: ' + data.numberOfNodes);
    console.log('-----------------------------
                      ----------------------');
  }
  phantom.exit(0);
});
```

In the preceding code, within the `evaluate()` function, we created a return in JSON type. JSON syntax in the simplest form must be enclosed within curly braces. The data within the curly braces must have a name followed by a colon, and then the value. Each pair must be delimited with a comma. For example:

```
{
    name: 'Tara',
    age: 10
}
```

To learn more about JSON, we can check out its main documentation site at `http://json.org/`.

The `evaluate()` function call returns the value of the title instead of a direct call to the `console.log()` function; the reason for this is that all calls for console message output will be suppressed. There is another technique available to do this, which will be discussed later on.

The data is returned and assigned to the receiving variable, which we then use to display on the web page. This completes our very simple example of retrieving a web page.

Playing with DOM elements

There are a lot of things we can do with the page we are accessing beyond getting the title of the document, and this can be done with a little help from the **Document Object Model** API. We are not going to discuss each object and function of the DOM API, but we will touch on some that are very useful. If you want to learn more about DOM API, the best place to start is the **Mozilla Development Network**: `https://developer.mozilla.org/en-US/docs/DOM`.

Selecting elements

Everything starts with the `document` object, and it contains nested elements. To select an element, we either traverse the entire document or use the DOM selectors. There are different methods to reference a document element, which can be done by element ID, class, name, tag, or XPath.

`getElementById`	This retrieves the element using a unique ID
`getElementByClassName`	This selects the element using the element class name
`getElementByName`	This provides a reference using the element name
`getElementByTagName`	This gets the element using the element tag name
`querySelector`	This searches for elements using the CSS selector

Each function is used depending on the scenario or document composition. We can use these functions as we normally do in JavaScript code; however, since we are going to access within the context of the page, we need to enclose the code with the `evaluate()` function of the `webpage` module.

```
var content = page.evaluate(function () {
    var element = document.querySelector('#elem1');
    return element.textContent;
});
console.log(content);
```

In the preceding code, based on the fetched page, we select the element with the ID `elem1`, extract the text content, and return it to display the data in our console.

Let's look at a real world example.

Pinterest is an exciting social media website, which allows you to share photos in a pinboard-style. Each user in Pinterest can have several boards and photo postings, and can follow social friends. With Pinterest's web profile, we can view user details in terms of how many photos are pinned, the number of boards created, total followers, and how many users are being followed.

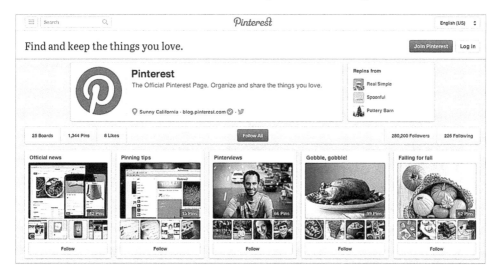

We want our script to accept one parameter, which is the Pinterest user ID. The first section of our script accepts that parameter. We use the `system` module to retrieve the parameter from the command line.

```
var system = require('system');
var userid = system.args[1];
var page = require('webpage').create();
```

Next, we open the user's page based on Pinterest's user profile URL at `http://www.pinterest.com/userid`.

We create a `page` object from the `webpage` module, then use `open()` to navigate to that page.

```
var profileUrl = "http://www.pinterest.com/" + userid;
    page.open(profileUrl, function(status) {
```

After the page is loaded, we now extract the information from the page. Let's get the number of pins first. We can use `querySelector` to select a certain part of the page and retrieve the content. However, from what we have learned previously, to retrieve and use DOM functions, we need to be in the context of the page, and use the `evaluate()` function of `webpage`.

But wait; how do we get that element ID that we will pass to `querySelector`? The only answer is to check the page's HTML source and inspect it. In most modern browsers. this is easily done.

In a Safari browser, simply right-click on a target element or text and select **Inspect Element**. It will show the ID or any unique identifier and will display the reference in the code.

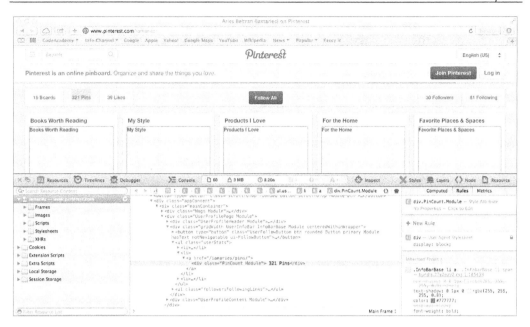

Based on the inspected DOM element, we can identify which form or path of the element we can use. Based on Pinterest's approach of creating the layout and how the details are presented, all the statistical data is put into the page with a clickable reference and are embedded using the `<a href>` element. With this information, we can use `querySelector` and lookup by the `href` attribute. The format for that will be as follows:

```
document.querySelector('[href="URL"]');
```

In the preceding example, we will replace URL with the proper href URL value, as we found in the web page. If we go back to our browser's investigate view and inspect the pins' text content, it will show us the URL value (see the following screenshot for more details):

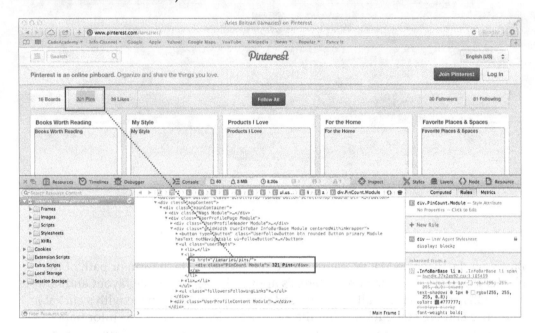

So, we can now use querySelector('[href="/iamaries/pins/"]') to get the number of pins for this user.

```
if ( status === "success" ) {
  var pinterest = page.evaluate(function () {
    var numberPins = document.querySelector
      ('[href="/iamaries/pins/"]').innerText.trim();

    return {
      pins: numberPins
    };
  });
```

Now with this code, we can get the number of pins for this user; however, this is only applicable for a specific user, since we hardcoded `href` with the specific user ID. Let's tweak a bit of our code and make it more flexible based on the passed user ID that we get as the argument. First, we need to add the `userid` variable that we have declared before and that holds the value based on the passed argument as the second parameter of `page.evaluate()`, as shown in the following code:

```
page.evaluate(function (uid) {
  // code content
}, userid);
```

The second and succeeding parameters of the `evaluate()` function denote the list of values we need to pass to the page context, as we now know that any other variables that we have cannot be referenced with the page context, as well as within the `evaluate()` function. You will also notice that our function callback definition does now have the `uid` parameter; this represents the value we passed from `userid`. Each extra parameter of `evaluate` should be passed as a parameter of the `function` callback for us to retrieve and reference the value.

Modify our code to have this concept applied as follows:

```
if ( status === "success" ) {
  var pinterest = page.evaluate(function (uid) {
    var numberPins = document.querySelector
      ('[href="/' + uid + '/pins/"]').innerText.trim();

    return {
      pins: numberPins
    };
  }, userid);
```

From the previous hardcoded user ID, we now have a parameterized user ID. With this, we can now construct the selector for a certain user. There are other items that we can retrieve and are able to display back, such as the number of boards, number of pins that the user likes, the number of followers, and the number of users that the user follows. Let's complete our Pinterest code.

```
var system = require('system');
var userid = system.args[1];
var page = require('webpage').create();

var profileUrl = "http://www.pinterest.com/" + userid;
  page.open(profileUrl, function(status) {
```

```
    if ( status === "success" ) {
      var pinterest = page.evaluate(function (uid) {
        var numberPins = document.querySelector
          ('[href="/' + uid + '/pins/"]').innerText.trim();
        var numberFollowers = document.querySelector
          ('[href="/' + uid + '/followers/"]').innerText.trim();
        var numberFollowing = document.querySelector
          ('[href="/' + uid + '/following/"]').innerText.trim();
        var numberBoards = document.querySelector
          ('[href="/' + uid + '/boards/"]').innerText.trim();
        var numberLikes = document.querySelector
          ('[href="/' + uid + '/likes/"]').innerText.trim();
        var userName = document.getElementsByClassName
          ("userProfileHeaderName").item(0).innerText.trim();

        return {
          name: userName,
          social: {
          followers: numberFollowers,
          following: numberFollowing
          },
          stats: {
          boards: numberBoards,
          pins: numberPins,
          likes: numberLikes
          }
        };
      }, userid);

      console.log(pinterest.name + ' has ' + pinterest.stats.pins +
                  ', ' + pinterest.stats.boards +
                  ', ' + pinterest.stats.likes +
                  ' with ' + pinterest.social.followers +
                  ' and ' + pinterest.social.following +
                  ' Awesome Users.');
    }

    phantom.exit(0);
});
```

Since there is a lot of data to be returned, it is better to return the data as a JSON object, as shown in the following code:

```
return {
  name: userName,
  social: {
    followers: numberFollowers,
    following: numberFollowing
  },
  stats: {
    boards: numberBoards,
    pins: numberPins,
    likes: numberLikes
  }
};
```

Now, let's use that object and display the output:

```
console.log(pinterest.name + ' has ' + pinterest.stats.pins +
            ', ' + pinterest.stats.boards +
            ', ' + pinterest.stats.likes +
            ' with ' + pinterest.social.followers +
            ' and ' + pinterest.social.following +
            ' Awesome Users.');
```

Our code is now complete. Let's try it by passing `pinterest` as our target user ID.

```
sources — bash — 120×14
$ phantomjs pinterest.js pinterest
Pinterest has 1,344 Pins, 25 Boards, 8 Likes with 280,264 Followers and 226 Following Awesome Users.

$
```

Using PhantomJS, we can extract certain information and process it, as demonstrated previously. The possibilities that can be done with the page context are relative to what you can do with the DOM API. We can modify the HTML code, content, attributes, and even change the CSS styling. Let's explore more and do some page interactions.

Simulating mouse clicks

Web pages are built with interlocking links, and getting to another page can be done by following that link. In a normal browser, this is done by clicking with your mouse button. In PhantomJS there are two ways to do this: one is by using PhantomJS `sendEvent` functions (PhantomJS event triggering); the other is by using DOM event triggering.

PhantomJS event triggering

The WebPage API supports sending events to the page. This can be mouse events or keyboard events. We will discuss more events as we progress, but for now we will tackle how to simulate clicking on page elements and links using PhantomJS event triggering.

PhantomJS Mouse Event Triggering API	
sendEvent (eventType, Point X, Point Y, button='left')	
eventType	• mouseup
	• mousedown
	• mousemove
	• click
	• doubleclick
Point X	This is the X coordinate where we trigger the event
Point Y	This is the Y coordinate where we trigger the event
button	This states which mouse button to trigger; by default, it is defined as the left mouse button

In PhantomJS, `sendEvent` triggers the event directly to the target container. It also relies on the x and y coordinates that are passed where the event should be originating; hence, it is like the user performing the actual event, such as a click.

Since we are not moving the mouse pointer to a certain clickable element, we need to identify the coordinate of the element where we intend to trigger the `click` event.

```
var system = require('system');
var url = system.args[1];
var page = require('webpage').create();
page.open('page1.htm', function(status) {
  if ( status === "success" ) {
    var point = page.evaluate(function () {
      var element = document.querySelector('#page2');
      var rect = element.getBoundingClientRect();
      return {
        x: rect.left + Math.floor(rect.width / 2),
        y: rect.top + (rect.height / 2)
      };
    });
    page.sendEvent('click', point.x, point.y);
    phantom.exit(0);
  }
});
```

In the preceding code, the `sendEvent` function is called, passing the `'click'` event type and having the coordinate based on the extracted value of a given element. Using the `getBoundingClientRect` function of the DOM element, we can access the rectangular bounds of the target element. Using this information, we can compute simply by dividing the `height` and `width` by 2 to get the center point of the element where we want to trigger the `click` event.

Before we run this code, let's first see the target HTML page, as shown in the following code:

```
<html>
  <head>
    <title>PhantomJS</title>
  </head>
  <body>
    <h1>Hello</h1>
    <a href='page2.htm' id='page2'>
      Go to Page 2
    </a>
  </body>
</html>
```

Our HTML is very simple. We have few elements on the page: a header element and the link element with `id` of `page2`, which we will use in our script as a reference.

Now let's test this code. The following will be the output:

```
$ ./phantomjs click01.js


$
```

So what happened? Technically, everything works perfectly; the page loaded and the element to be clicked received the event. To make it more visual, we will add the code to inform us that the element was clicked.

Let's add an alert notification when the element is clicked. A simple inline JavaScript on the element will be sufficient.

```
<h1>Hello</h1>
<a href='page2.htm' id='page2' onclick='alert("Clicked.")'>
  Go to Page 2
</a>
```

In the preceding code, we added the `onclick` event handler. It will only display an alert message when the element is clicked.

Since PhantomJS is a headless browser, there will be no dialog box popping up on the screen; rather, it will generate a related event. This event can be handled and we can retrieve the message that is supposed to be displayed. To do this, we override the `onAlert` event of the `webpage` instance.

```
var page = require('webpage').create();

page.onAlert = function(msg) {
  console.log(msg);
};

page.open('page1.htm', function(status) {
```

In the preceding code, we added a new handler for `onAlert`. The function definition has a single parameter which passes the message to be displayed in an alert box. We then implement simple handling such as displaying the message to the console using the `log` function.

Let's try running our script again. This should display the alert message if we successfully clicked the element.

```
$ ./phantomjs click02.js
Clicked.


$
```

Ta da! The element did receive the click event. So let's try using another approach of clicking the element.

DOM event triggering

As an alternative, we can use the DOM event approach for sending mouse events. To do this, first we need to have the element reference, as we did in the previous example.

```
var element = document.querySelector('#page2');
```

After that, we create a new mouse event using the DOM `createEvent` function.

```
var evt = document.createEvent("MouseEvents");
```

Using the newly created event object, we initialize the mouse event property as follows:

```
evt.initMouseEvent(
  "click",       // Event Type
  true,
  true,
  window,
  1,
  1, 1, 1, 1,   // Screen and Client Coordinate Points
  false,        // Ctrl Key Modifier
  false,        // Alt Key Modifier
  false,        // Shift Key Modifier
  false,        // Meta Key Modifier
  0,            // Mouse Button
  element);     // Target Element
```

Lastly, we dispatch the event.

```
element.dispatchEvent(evt);
```

This should result in the same output as the PhantomJS event triggering. The DOM coding is the same as the one you normally use in your JavaScript code.

 For more information on **Document Object Model Events**, please visit `http://www.w3.org/TR/DOM-Level-2-Events/events.html`

Working with form fields

If we are dealing with web pages, more often than not, we will come across form fields, which are input boxes, selection lists, text areas, and buttons. PhantomJS can also be used to automate the input of data and changing field values.

One of the best examples of these scenarios is a login page. We will create a script that will automate the login process to Instagram's web profile. Again, the username and password will be passed as command-line arguments. The first argument is `username`, followed by `password`.

```
var system = require('system');
var username = system.args[1];
var password = system.args[2];
```

Now that we have our credentials, we then open Instagram's login page at `https://www.instagram.com/accounts/login`.

```
var page = require('webpage').create();
page.open('https://instagram.com/accounts/login/',
function(status) {
```

With simple browser page inspection, we can check the element ID of the `username` field, `password` field, and `form` ID.

In the following code, using the DOM selection function, we retrieve the reference to the username field. This element is an instance of HTMLInputElement, since it is a definition of the <input> element.

```
▶ <header>…</header>
▼ <div class="dialog-main">
  ▼ <form method="POST" id="login-form" class="adjacent" action="/accounts/login/">
      <input type="hidden" name="csrfmiddlewaretoken" value=
      "e8c80fa6afeb48cad06dcd9e11d71b96">
    ▼ <p>
        <label for="id_username">Username:</label>
        <input name="username" maxlength="30" autocapitalize="off" autocorrect="off"
        type="text" id="id_username">
      </p>
    ▶ <p>…</p>
    ▶ <p class="form-actions">…</p>
    </form>
```

```
page.evaluate(function (uid, pwd) {
  var username_field = document.getElementById('id_username');
  username_field.value = uid;
  var password_field = document.getElementById('id_password');
  password_field.value = pwd;

  var form = document.getElementById('login-form');
  this.render('login.png');
  form.submit();
}, username, password);
```

We will be working again in the context of the web page, so we enclose all other page manipulation within the evaluate() function.

There are several attributes and functions that are defined for HTMLInputElement. Please refer to the **Mozilla Developer Network** DOM API documentation for further details.

We set the new value of the username field by setting the value attribute of the HTMLInputElement interface. The username that was passed from the command line is assigned to the value attribute of the element. The same approach is used for the password field. If the browser is shown, both fields should have the data typed in the input boxes. We can add screen capture code (as shown in the preceding code, just before the submission of the form) to render the current status of the input boxes that are filled up for us to see it visually happening. If we are to run the script, it should create a login.png image file to capture and show that the boxes are inserted with values.

To complete our login script, we need to submit the form. Forms are also elements that can be referenced. Form elements are objects based on HTMLFormElement, and this object has a submit() function to trigger the form submission.

The following is our complete script code:

```
var system = require('system');
var username = system.args[1];
var password = system.args[2];
var page = require('webpage').create();
page.open('https://instagram.com/accounts/login/',
function(status) {
  if ( status === "success" ) {
    page.evaluate(function (uid, pwd) {
      var username_field = document.getElementById('id_username');
      username_field.value = uid;
      var password_field = document.getElementById('id_password');
      password_field.value = pwd;

      var form = document.getElementById('login-form');
      this.render('login.png');
      form.submit();
    }, username, password);
  }
  phantom.exit(0);
});
```

Running the script will log in to Instagram's secured page using the credentials passed as arguments. The preceding script's output is as follows:

```
$ ./phantomjs login.js username password


$
```

Did we really get in and pass the authentication? Yes, we did. However, since most of the page loading takes place after you submit the form, based on our preceding code, the login process will be triggered but terminated. It is terminated because PhantomJS already receives the exit call right after submit().

When submit() is executed, a new page is requested and the loading of the next page starts in the background. As we all know, sometimes it takes a few seconds before everything is rendered after logging in.

To fix this, we need to pause the script and let PhantomJS finish loading the next page before calling the exit call. There is no built-in function to pause, so we are going to use the JavaScript setTimeout as a way of pausing the script process.

We replace the exit call using the following snippet, assuming that the login process will take about 3 seconds to complete, however, this depends on your network speed:

```
setTimeout( function() {
  phantom.exit(0);
}, 3000 );
```

Rather than exiting, we will force a 3 second or a 3000 millisecond pause in our script to let the loading happen in the background. After reaching 3 seconds, the code inside the function() callback will be performed where we placed our exit call.

To test if we really logged in, we can assert specific text or information that is found on the page after login, or we can also check if there is an error message that is shown; if yes, the login fails. The following is the page that shows an error message if an attempt to log in fails:

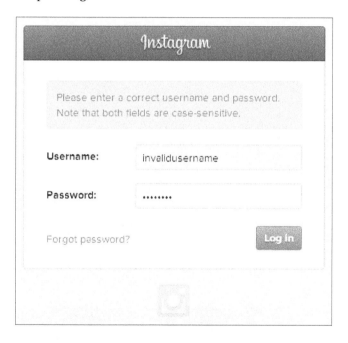

The error message in Instagram's login page is dynamic, and will only be available if an error occurs. We can inspect the error page and get the reference element that holds this message, using it as our way for checking if we are able to log in successfully.

In the error page, an element with a class ID of `alert-red` will be present if an error occurs. So instead of exiting, we can insert code that will check if that element is present in the current page content. If it is, we can tell that the login failed.

```
setTimeout( function() {
  var error = page.evaluate(function(){
    var error = document.querySelector('.alert-red');
    var error_message = false;
    if( error != null) {
      error_message = document.querySelector
        ('.alert-red').innerText.trim();
    }

    return error_message;
  });
  page.render("login2.png");

  if(!error) {
    console.log('Login Successful');
  } else {
    console.log('Login Failed: ' + error);
  }

  phantom.exit(0);
}, 5000 );
```

In the preceding code, we also retrieve the error message and display it back to the console, and after the checking the result page, we can capture the page at its current state so that we can visually check it after we run our script.

Running our script with an invalid username and password will give us the following output:

```
sources — bash — 120×14
$ phantomjs login.js invalid password
Login Failed: Please enter a correct username and password. Note that both fields are case-sensitive.

$
```

Summary

PhantomJS's capability of manipulating web pages is very flexible. We can do a lot more than just accessing the page itself. We can modify the look, change content on the fly, or even dynamically interact with its behavior as it was coded. In this chapter, we have tried to capture relevant data from an existing social media site and use it for any other purpose. This is just the beginning of what PhantomJS can do as far as interacting with web pages. We also touched a bit upon handling the status of pages and did a simple pausing. Using JavaScript's setTimeout is just a simple workaround to let the background process complete. Proper handling of page events is also supported in PhantomJS, and we will be discussing them in the next chapter.

3
Handling Events and Callbacks

A browser adapts based on user-driven events—these can be mouse or key events. A browser reacts by doing something when these events are received. Events are not only generated by the user as there are also events that are triggered and received by the application, such as an incoming message alert, a request to pick up a file, or incoming data packets over the network. PhantomJS has several webpage callbacks that we can listen to in order to perform additional processing when these events are received.

Listening to page events

Unlike a real browser, where we can see the page events happening visually, in PhantomJS, we cannot see anything. For example, on a real browser, we can see the status bar of the browser changing from one message to another when loading subpages and resources; we can also see that the images and text are slowly showing up as the entire page is being rendered by the browser. In PhantomJS, we can get information when these events and callbacks are handled appropriately.

Page load events

There are two events that are related to page loading: `onLoadStarted` and `onLoadFinsihed`. You can attach callbacks to the page object for each event.

The `onLoadStarted` event will be triggered when PhantomJS starts loading the page based on the resources received. The function takes no parameters. It is just a signal that the loading process has started.

```
page.onLoadStarted = function() {
  console.log("Page Loading Started");
};
```

When the page load is complete, another event will be triggered, and we can catch this by overriding the `onLoadFinished` event. Unlike `onLoadStarted`, the event passes a single parameter that holds the status of the page loading. The value of the parameter will hold the same status that we get from `page.open()`.

```
page.onLoadFinished = function(status) {
    console.log("Page Loaded: " + status);
};
```

Using a simple page open, handling these two events will give us two console prints: **Page Loading Started** which is displayed first, followed by **Page Loaded**.

```
var system = require('system');
var url = system.args[1];

var page = require('webpage').create();
page.onLoadStarted = function () {
    console.log('Page Loading Started');
};

page.onLoadFinished = function () {
    console.log('Page Loaded');
    phantom.exit(0);
};

page.open(url);
```

Expect the following result when our script is executed:

```
$ ./phantomjs pageload.js http://www.google.com
Page Load Started
Page Loaded
```

That was easy. Let us try to improve this by adding a load time measurement. First, in our `onLoadStarted` function, we will keep the start time.

```
var startTime = null;
page.onLoadStarted = function() {
    startTime = new Date().getTime();
}
```

In the preceding code, we created a `startTime` variable, which will hold the timestamp when the `onLoadStarted` function is triggered, and during this event, we pass the current time to our variable.

In the `onLoadFinished` function, we also get the current time, and then we subtract this from the variable that we kept during the `onLoadStarted` function. We can do this by calculating the difference between the end time and start time. The resulting value will be in milliseconds.

```
page.onLoadFinished = function () {
  endTime = new Date().getTime();
  timeInSeconds = (endTime - startTime) / 1000;
  console.log("Loading takes " + timeInSeconds + " seconds.");
  phantom.exit(0);
};
```

Running our script will give us the time elapsed in loading the URL that we requested.

```
$ ./phantomjs pageload2.js http://www.google.com
Loading takes 0.581 seconds.
```

You will notice that the `exit` method was also called within our `onLoadFinshed` function, rather than after the page `open` call. This is to prevent the premature termination of our script. If we add the `exit` method right after the `open` method, the `open` method call will be processed asynchronously, and PhantomJS will execute the next command immediately. Thus, the process of loading will be interrupted and the script will be terminated. To solve this problem, we will only terminate the script upon completion of everything (inside the `onLoadFinished` handler).

The page loading measurement is more complex than page start and page end, since there are subpages and other resources like cascading style sheets, images, and external JavaScript files. We can also measure the time spent in loading each resource, using other page events that PhantomJS supports. The `onResourceRequested` and `onResourceReceived` events can be overridden to handle resource-related events that are generated within the page loading.

When a resource is requested

Both, the main page resource and other resources that are embedded within the page are requested during the page loading; each of them will trigger an event of resource requested. This can be monitored with the `onResourceRequested` event handler.

```
page.onResourceRequested = function (request) {
  console.log('Resource Requested');
};
```

The `onResourceRequested` callback function passes the request object, which contains the details of the resource being requested for retrieval from the host server. The `request` object is in JSON format.

```
{
  "headers": [
  {
    "name": "User-Agent",
            "value": "Mozilla/5.0 (Windows NT 6.1; WOW64)
            AppleWebKit/534.34 (KHTML, like Gecko) PhantomJS/1.6.0
            Safari/534.34"
  },
  {
    "name": "Referer",
    "value": "http://www.google.com.ph/"
  },
  {
    "name": "Accept",
    "value": "*/*"
  }
  ],
  "id": 7,
  "method": "GET",
  "time": "2013-02-14T08:39:01.160Z",
  "url": http://clients1.google.com.ph/generate_204
}
```

The preceding code is an example of the request object passed to `onResourceRequested`. The object contains the necessary information that we can use to measure the resource loading time. Let us try to create a simple `onResourceRequested` implementation, and display the information we can get out of the `request` object:

```
page.onResourceRequested = function (request) {
  console.log('Resource Requested');
  console.log('-------------------------------------------');
  console.log('Id     : ' + request.id);
  console.log('URL    : ' + request.url);
  console.log('Method : ' + request.method);
  console.log('-------------------------------------------');
  console.log('Headers');
  console.log('-------------------------------------------');
  request.headers.forEach(function(header){
    console.log(header.name + ' = ' + header.value);
  });
  console.log('-------------------------------------------');
};
```

We can access each of the values from the `request` object using the name of the item by directly referencing it, using the `request` object, followed by a dot character, and then the name of the item as shown in line the preceding code.

Within the `request` object, all HTTP request headers for this request are also included as another collection. We can retrieve that by referencing the `headers` name. Since `request.headers` is a collection, we can also use the traversal method of displaying or reading the object. Take a look at the preceding code for an example.

Alternatively, we can also use the `JSON.stringify()` method to format and display the request object. `JSON.stringify()` converts an object to a JSON string.

```
page.onResourceRequested = function (request) {
  console.log(JSON.stringify(request, null, 4));
};
```

We can also format the string, converted by passing the third parameter of the function, with any number of spaces used to indent each pair. We can learn more about this function by checking out the documentation available at: `https://developer.mozilla.org/en-US/docs/Web/JavaScript/Reference/Global_Objects/JSON/stringify`.

Normally, we do get multiple resource requests on a single page open. These requests are resources that are references within the page, such as images, external scripts, and style sheets. So, we can expect multiple resource request events, and our event handler code must be flexible enough to handle each unique request appropriately. The resource requested event will be called singularly, but this does not guarantee an immediate callback with `onResourceReceived`. PhantomJS will start a request and then trigger `onResourceRequest` in parallels. Due to the possibility of having multiple requests simultaneously, receiving the requested resource depends on the response time of the server.

Receiving a page resource

For each request, there will be another event that is triggered: `onResourceReceived`. This happens when PhantomJS receives the requested resource. The callback function is called along with a `response` object. Unlike the `request` object, the `response` object contains actual details of the requested URL. Some of the data is the status of the request, the actual size of the stream received, the content type, the size of the resource, and the header information:

```
page.onResourceReceived = function (response) {
  console.log('Resource Received');
};
```

With each request event, the resource receive event will be called in two stages: `start` and `end`. This means that the `onResourceReceived` function will be called twice for each resource. The `response` object has minor differences between stages. The start `response` object mostly contains the characteristic of the resource, while the end `response` defines the status of the request.

The following code is the `response` object for the start stage:

```
{
    "bodySize": 1039,
    "contentType": "image/png",
    "headers": [
    {
      "name": "Content-Type",
      "value": "image/png"
    },
    {
      "name": "Last-Modified",
      "value": "Fri, 09 Nov 2012 21:19:30 GMT"
    },
    {
      "name": "Date",
      "value": "Wed, 13 Feb 2013 22:26:50 GMT"
    },
    {
      "name": "Expires",
      "value": "Thu, 21 Feb 2013 22:26:50 GMT"
    },
    {
      "name": "X-Content-Type-Options",
      "value": "nosniff"
    },
    {
      "name": "Server",
      "value": "sffe"
    },
    {
      "name": "Content-Length",
      "value": "35615"
    },
    {
      "name": "X-XSS-Protection",
      "value": "1; mode=block"
    },
```

```
    {
      "name": "Cache-Control",
      "value": "public, max-age=691200"
    },
    {
      "name": "Age",
      "value": "61934"
    }
    ],
    "id": 5,
    "redirectURL": null,
    "stage": "start",
    "status": 200,
    "statusText": "OK",
    "time": "2013-02-14T15:44:26.895Z",
    "url": http://www.google.com.ph/images/srpr/nav_logo80.png
  }
```

And, the following JSON data is the end stage for the `response` object:

```
  {
    "contentType": "image/png",
    "headers": [
    {
      "name": "Content-Type",
      "value": "image/png"
    },
    {
      "name": "Last-Modified",
      "value": "Fri, 09 Nov 2012 21:19:30 GMT"
    },
    {
      "name": "Date",
      "value": "Wed, 13 Feb 2013 22:26:50 GMT"
    },
    {
      "name": "Expires",
      "value": "Thu, 21 Feb 2013 22:26:50 GMT"
    },
    {
      "name": "X-Content-Type-Options",
      "value": "nosniff"
    },
    {
```

```
      "name": "Server",
      "value": "sffe"
    },
    {
      "name": "Content-Length",
      "value": "35615"
    },
    {
      "name": "X-XSS-Protection",
      "value": "1; mode=block"
    },
    {

      "name": "Cache-Control",
      "value": "public, max-age=691200"
    },
    {
      "name": "Age",
      "value": "61934"
    }
    ],
    "id": 5,
    "redirectURL": null,
    "stage": "end",
    "status": 200,
    "statusText": "OK",
    "time": "2013-02-14T15:44:28.047Z",
    "url": "http://www.google.com.ph/images/srpr/nav_logo80.png"
}
```

Both the `response` objects contain an attribute of a stage, indicating which stage the response belongs to. Using this attribute, we can filter the data coming from the `onResourceReceived` callback.

Two stages of the resource received event

The start stage and the end stage complete a full resource received process. When PhantomJS starts a request of a URL to the server (which also triggers the `onResourceRequest` event), it waits until the server responds. The server won't respond immediately with a full stream of data. It will, however, inform the client (which is PhantomJS) the details of the incoming stream, and this denotes our resource is received (start stage), and PhantomJS will trigger an event, as illustrated in the following figure:

After the `start` stage event is triggered, PhantomJS will now read the incoming data stream. The `end` stage will be triggered once the stream is completed. In this event, we will receive a callback of `onResourceReceived` with a `stage` value of `"end"`. With these events, we can capture the wait time from request to response, and we can also time the actual streaming of data, which is very useful when doing a benchmarking or monitoring of page loads.

Let us finish up our load timing script. We now need to define our `onResourceRequested` callback function, and save the request data using the request `id` as our key:

```
var resources = [];

page.onResourceRequested = function (request) {
  resource = {
    "startTime": request.time,
    "url": request.url
  };
  resources[request.id] = resource;
};
```

Firstly, we define a new array and name it `resources`. This will hold details for each resource. We will use `id`, so that we can match the details when we receive events from `onResourceReceived`. This `id` will be unique during the page loading process, so we are sure that the resource being referenced on received is the one that we have saved during the request. The `id` variable will also act as the index in our `resources` variable, as shown in the preceding code. We can save all of the information within the `response` object, but for simplicity in our example, we will just keep the time and the URL.

Since we have a reference for the requested URL, we can now handle the incoming resource in the `onResourceReceived` callback function.

```
page.onResourceReceived = function (response) {
    if(response.stage == "start") {
      resources[response.id].size = response.bodySize;
    } else if(response.stage == "end") {
      resources[response.id].endTime = response.time;
    }
};
```

In the resource received callback, we want to save the timestamp when the resource was received, and we do that during the end stage. We will use this to extract the time difference between the time received and the time recorded during the request. If we want to know the size of the resource, we can do that during the start stage, where the body size of the stream is defined. The size is in bytes.

The last step that is needed is to output what we have gathered, and we want this output after all things are completed. As we learned earlier, we will process and compute for each resource loading time when the page loading is finished.

```
page.onLoadFinished = function () {
    endTime = new Date();
    timeInSeconds = (endTime - startTime) / 1000;
    console.log("Loading takes " + timeInSeconds + " seconds.");

    resources.forEach(function (resource) {
      st = new Date(resource.startTime).getTime();
      et = new Date(resource.endTime).getTime();
      timeSpent = (et - st) / 1000;
      console.log(timeSpent + " seconds : "  + resource.url);
    });

    phantom.exit(0);
};
```

We traverse our array of resources using `forEach`. Since we appropriately handled each request and receive event, we should have the data matching for each requested resource.

Each resource has its own start and end time. We extract that and convert the time into milliseconds and derive the difference. And lastly, we output the time in seconds along with the resource URL.

Our script should have the following output:

```
$ ./phantomjs pageload3.js http://www.google.com
Loading takes 6.751 seconds.
0.255 seconds : http://www.google.com/
0.379 seconds : http://www.google.com.ph/
0.213 seconds : http://ssl.gstatic.com/gb/images/b_8d5afc09.png
0.676 seconds : http://www.google.com.ph/images/srpr/logo1w.png
0.561 seconds : http://www.google.com.ph/images/srpr/nav_logo80.png
6.135 seconds : http://www.google.com.ph/xjs/_/js/hp/sb_he,pcc/rt=j/ver=_
aDh7zAWqI8.en_US./d=1/sv=1/rs=AItRSTOgg467Qcx4GftzMMz3ZDPd841cog
```

If you carefully evaluate the output, you will find that the total loading time is much shorter than the summation of all time spent loading each resource. PhantomJS loads each resource asynchronously, and there are resources that are being loaded simultaneously.

There are several uses for this kind of script. One is we can save each run of the script into a series of runtimes, and eventually generate a graph to monitor the performance of our web applications. PhantomJS also provides an example at `https://github.com/ariya/phantomjs/tree/master/examples`, demonstrating the same idea of network sniffing and saving the output into the **HTTP Archive (HAR)** format.

Try modifying the script and adding the size of the resources along with the time-load duration. You can play around with this and measure the wait time of the request until the server starts to send a data stream back.

Knowing when the URL changes

To keep track of the URL changes within the script execution, we can handle that process using the `onUrlChanged` function. This function passes a string, which contains the new URL to be navigated.

```
page.onUrlChanged = function(url) {
  console.log('Change to: ' + url);
};
```

This event will be triggered when the page instance URL changes. This also applies to the first URL we open.

Now, we know when the URL has changed, but not the method used to navigate to the new URL. PhantomJS also provides the `onNavigationRequested` callback, which gives us more information by passing some details to this function. This event also occurs before the `onUrlChanged` function.

```
page.onNavigationRequested = function(url, type,
  willNavigate, main) {
  if(willNavigate) {
    console.log("Navigating to " + url + " which is
      triggered by " + type + ".");
  } else {
    console.log("Navigate is not permitted.");
  }
};
```

Capturing alert messages

It is common for most web developers to display a message using the JavaScript alert message box. These are pop-up messages that are displayed on top of the browser. Since we are running a headless browser, these pop ups will not be seen, but rest assured that they are triggered. We can still capture these events using the webpage `onAlert()`.

```
var page = require('webpage').create();

page.onAlert = function(msg) {
  console.log(msg);
};
```

In the preceding code, we had overridden the `onAlert` callback after we created an instance of the web page module. The function receives a single parameter, which contains the message intended to be displayed in the pop-up message box. The function process that we provided here will be used by all alert messages — we can consume the message and display it to our console, or we can capture and save it as a list of messages received.

Answering prompt messages

Aside from alert messages, there are prompt messages that ask users to input their answer into a single text field. To handle this kind of dialog box from web pages, PhantomJS allows us to handle and answer back to this dialog prompts using the `onPrompt` callback.

```
page.onPrompt = function(message, defaultVal) {
  if (message === 'How old are you?') {
    return '18';
  }

  return defaultVal;
};
```

The `onPrompt` function callback receives two parameters. The first parameter is the message to be displayed in the prompt dialog; this normally asks a question back to the user. The second parameter is the default value or answer.

Responding to confirm pop ups - OK or Cancel

The `onConfirm` function in JavaScript displays pop ups which ask the user for an action that is answerable by either yes or no. The `onConfirm` function callback allows us to respond to this pop-up dialog box.

```
page.onConfirm = function(msg) {
  return true;
};
```

The callback function has a single parameter, which contains the question being asked to the user. We respond to this pop up by returning either `true` or `false`. For example, we want to click the `OK` button, then we return `true`; otherwise we return `false`.

There are several more callback functions that you can use to listen and handle page events within PhantomJS. We can also catch error messages that are encountered during running the script. We will learn more about error handling in the next chapter.

Performing user events

In some cases, we will need to emulate user keyboard events and mouse events. PhantomJS provides a simple function to trigger these events from our script. These events will provide necessary actions in our script, from clicking on a URL to inputting usernames and passwords, or just filling up a form.

The function `sendEvent`, from the WebPage API, has the capability to perform these events on the page from our scripts.

```
page.sendEvent(eventType[,event specific arguments])
```

There are two types of events that are supported: keyboard and mouse events. Each event differs by the set of arguments that can be passed to the functions to match the necessary data to perform the event.

Keyboard events

Let us first explore how to use key events. The following is the complete function signature for the key event.

```
page.sendEvent(keyEventType, keyOrKeys, null, null, modifier).
```

The key event type can be either `'keypress'`, `'keydown'`, or `'keyup'`. The second argument can be a single character or a string of characters. We can reference and use the `page.event.key` object for built-in constants. We can use the `page.event.key.A` for capital letter A, or `page.event.key.F1` for triggering the *F1* key. Check the *Appendix* for a list of key constants.

The third and fourth argument is unused, and we can just leave it `null`. The last argument is the key event modifier, which can be a combination of key modifiers.

Key modifier	
No modifier	0
Shift key	0x02000000
Ctrl key	0x04000000
Alt key	0x08000000
Meta key	0x10000000
Keypad button	0x20000000

So, if we are supposed to be sending *Ctrl + Shift + Page Down*, we can call that in our script by using the following code:

```
page.sendEvent('keypress', page.event.key.PageDown,
                null, null,
                0x04000000 | 0x02000000)
```

If we are to visit a page capable of using keys as a shortcut to navigate around the page, like Gmail, for instance, then this will be very useful. We will create a new script that will send these shortcut-keyboard events; however, we will not use Gmail in our example. We will have our own little page that has the capability to display which key was pressed. First, we build up our test page which we will run our PhantomJS script with. We will use jQuery to bind the key events to our page using the following script:

```
$(window).keyup(function(event) {
  addEntry(event);
  event.preventDefault();
  return false;
});

function addEntry(event) {
  var data = "<tr><td>" +
              event.type      + "</td><td>" +
              event.keyCode   + "</td><td>" +
              event.ctrlKey   + "</td><td>" +
              event.altKey    + "</td><td>" +
              event.shiftKey  + "</td><td>" +
              event.metaKey   + "</td></tr>";
  $('#keyEventsBody > tbody:last').append(data);
}
```

The preceding code is for our test page, and using jQuery we will set up a handler when a `keyup` function is generated within the page. Our test is to check if the emulated key events from the PhantomJS script will be recognized by our test page. We can add two more event capturing handlers for key down and for key press. The following is the script in PhantomJS:

```
var system = require('system');
var page = require('webpage').create();

page.open('keyevents.htm', function(status) {
  if ( status === "success" ) {
    page.render('beforekey.png');
```

```
    // sending arrow left key
    page.sendEvent('keypress',
                page.event.key.Left,
                null, null, 0);

    // sending Ctrl+A
    page.sendEvent('keypress',
                page.event.key.A,
                null, null, 0x04000000);
    page.render('afterkey.png');
    phantom.exit(0);
  }
});
```

In the preceding code, first we load the test page, then after loading, we capture a screenshot, which should render just the header of the test page. Then, we emulate the key events using the sendEvent function. And finally, we capture the page screen again. In the second screenshot, we expect that this will generate and display the captured events. The following is a sample screenshot:

PhantomJS Capture Key Events

Key Event	Key	Control	Alt	Shift	Meta

Before sendEvent

PhantomJS Capture Key Events

Key Event	Key	Control	Alt	Shift	Meta
keydown	65	false	false	false	false
keyup	65	false	false	false	false
keydown	37	false	false	false	false
keyup	37	false	false	false	false

After sendEvent

We can use these methods not only for navigation or hotkeys, but also for filling up forms. Especially, on form fields that have JavaScript triggers when the value or a key event is bounded, instead of manipulating the field value and changing them directly.

Mouse events

Aside from key events, we can also emulate mouse events such as `mouseup`, `mousedown`, `mousemove`, `click`, and `doubleclick`.

```
page.sendEvent(mouseEventType, mouseX, mouseY, button='left')
```

The second and third argument will have the coordinates to which the event will occur relative to the page. The last argument is the button that is triggered when the event occurs; by default, it is set to `'left'`.

```
var point = page.evaluate(function () {
  var element = document.querySelector('#button1');
  var rect = element.getBoundingClientRect();
  return {
    x: rect.left + Math.floor(rect.width / 2),
    y: rect.top + (rect.height / 2)
  };
});
page.sendEvent('click', point.x, point.y);
```

The preceding code is a snippet where a button needs to be clicked. Here, we tried to access the `#button1` element by selecting it from our page. In the line following this, we extract the bounding boundaries of the element using the `getBoundingClientRect` function. This function will return an object based on the element's location in a page, which can be found using its coordinates and size.

Then, we compute the button's middle point and return it as a JSON object. This coordinate will be used for emulating the mouse click. Whatever code or event that is bound for that button will be performed as if the user physically clicked the mouse device.

Webpage events are easily emulated or captured in PhantomJS. Using our script, we can actually perform automated web browsing with anticipated possible event scenarios, which will give us more ways to perform web testing and scraping. Along with this, PhantomJS also allows us to trigger user events such as keyboard and mouse events, which will give us more ways to create simulated scenario test. In the next chapter, we will learn how to capture errors that affect PhantomJS and our script.

Summary

This chapter shows how to tap into the PhantomJS capability of handling and triggering different events. We have covered different aspects like handling page events and callbacks, sending keyboard events, and simulating mouse events. In the next chapter, we will learn the details on how to capture error messages.

4
Capturing Errors

Sometimes, we will encounter unexpected problems that generate errors triggered by PhantomJS scripts or from the page itself. There are several ways to handle errors and exceptions in our script; we can use callbacks that are readily available in PhantomJS or through JavaScript exception handling. More often, we combine both to have a much better way of capturing errors.

Handling PhantomJS errors

PhantomJS scripts are not compiled, so we do expect that both runtime- and syntax-related errors could be thrown during script execution. These types of errors can be handled using the `phantom` object's `onError` callback.

If PhantomJS encounters a syntax error in the script, it will call the function defined for this callback; if there is no function defined for this callback, it will perform the default implementation and output the errors in the console as shown in the following screenshot:

```
                          sources — bash — 120×14
$ phantomjs ch4_0.js
TypeError: 'undefined' is not a function (evaluating 'phantom.hello()')

   ch4_0.js:9 in say
   ch4_0.js:12
```

PhantomJS will display the error message followed by a series of lines, which denotes the stack of the error call. It will also display the function or method with a source line number.

This information is also passed to any function that we've defined for the `onError` callback. The `onError` callback definition is as follows:

```
phantom.onError = function(msg, trace) {
    // code handling
};
```

The `onError` callback will accept two parameters as shown in the preceding code. The first parameter is the error message, which is in the string format. The code stack trace is the second parameter. This object is an array that contains the following attribute of each item:

Stack trace item attributes	Description
function	The name of the function where the error originated.
file	The name of the file or script.
sourceURL	The source URL of the script. This is omitted if the file is present.
line	The line number where the error occurred.

Let's re-implement the `onError` function and slightly modify the default error output.

```
phantom.onError = function(msg, trace) {
    console.log(msg);
    if (trace) {
        trace.forEach(function(t) {
            var stackmsg = '  at' + (t.function ? ' function ' +
                                     t.function : '') +
                            ' (' + (t.file || t.sourceURL) + ':' +
                            t.line + ')';
            console.log(stackmsg);
        });
    }
};
```

First, we display the actual error message as you can see in the preceding code. Then, we check whether or not the code stack trace is present by checking whether or not the trace parameter object can be converted to the true value. If we do have the stack trace object, we iterate it as an array of trace items. We will display the function, if present, and then the script file or the source URL, and then, finally, the line number associated with it.

Truthy and Falsy

JavaScript objects have an inherent Boolean value; this means that everything in JavaScript can be converted to either `true` or `false`. We might come across some of these comparisons and conversions all throughout the book and these few reminders might help a bit. All of the following values are converted to falsy or false:

- `false`
- `0`
- `null`
- `undefined`
- `NaN`
- empty strings `" "`

All other objects are converted to truthy, including empty functions, empty arrays, empty objects, and string literals `0` and `false`.

Running the script would give us a slightly different output from the PhantomJS default behavior.

```
$ phantomjs ch4_1.js page1.htm
TypeError: 'undefined' is not a function (evaluating 'phantom.hello()')
  at function say (ch4_1.js:19)
  at (ch4_1.js:22)
```

The following code is based on the example script specified in the preceding screenshot:

```
var system = require('system');
var url = system.args[1];

phantom.onError = function(msg, trace) {
  console.log(msg);
  if (trace) {
    trace.forEach(function(t) {
      var stackmsg = '  at' + (t.function ? ' function ' +
                              t.function : '') +
                ' (' + (t.file || t.sourceURL) +
                ':' + t.line + ')';
      console.log(stackmsg);
    });
  }
};
var page = require('webpage').create();
page.open(url);
function say() {
  phantom.hello();
}
say();
```

The script contains a method call to an unknown function, as seen in the preceding code. The `hello` function is not present in PhantomJS's `phantom` object. This will generate an error event, which will trigger the `onError` callback.

We don't normally display the error stack trace in our application, but rather, suppress them from the screen and write the details to a logfile, which we will do later on.

Capturing page script errors

Errors that are generated within the scripts that are coded within the `page.evaluate` method will not trigger `phantom.onError`; however, the `webpage` object's `onError` callback will receive the event instead. The definition of the function is the same, except that we define our handling on the `webpage` instance as shown in the following code:

```
var page = require('webpage').create();
page.onError = function(msg, trace) {
  console.log(msg);
```

```
    if (trace) {
      trace.forEach(function(t) {
        var stackmsg = '  at' + (t.function ? ' function '
                                  + t.function : '')
                    + ' (' + (t.file || t.sourceURL) + ':'
                       + t.line + ')';
        console.log(stackmsg);
      });
    }
};
```

Assume that we have the following code in our `webpage` evaluate block:

```
page.open(url, function(status) {
  page.evaluate(function() {
    documentx.content = 1;
  });
});
```

As we see in the preceding code, we have a reference to an object named `documentx`, which is an invalid object since there is no such object within the page (see `page1.html` of the following code).

```
<html>
  <head>
    <title>Page 1</title>
  </head>
  <body>
    <h1>Page 1</h1>
    <a href='page2.htm' id='page2'>Go to Page 2</a>
  </body>
</html>
```

When we execute this script, it will generate an error and call the `page.onError` handling. The phantom object definition will not be called since it is beyond the scope of the `webpage` object, as shown in the following screenshot:

Since the `documentx` object is unknown, it will generate a reference error stating that the variable cannot be found. This error handling is not limited to the `evaluate` block codes. This callback will also receive error events if the page being referenced contains JavaScript errors.

Let us say we have `pagex.htm` and that the following will be the HTML source:

```
<html>
  <head>
    <title>Page X</title>
    <script>
      $('#not_an_element').show();
    </script>
  </head>
  <body>
    <h1>Page X</h1>
  </body>
</html>
```

In the preceding code, we have a JavaScript code that uses a third-party library syntax, which we did not include previously; because of this, the syntax is not recognized and will generate an error upon loading the page. Running our preceding script and loading `pagex.htm` will show the output shown in the following screenshot:

```
$ phantomjs ch4_3.js pagex.htm
ReferenceError: Can't find variable: $
  at (file:///book/chapter4/sources/pagex.htm:5)
```

Anticipating the page loading error

Since we will soon be dealing with page loading, we should have some capabilities to identify whether or not the page is properly loaded. We can do this by checking the status of the loading of the page using the `webpage` object's `open` callback.

```
var system = require('system');
var url = system.args[1];
```

```
var page = require('webpage').create();
page.open(url, function(status) {
  if(status == 'success') {
    console.log('Page loaded.');
    // do more stuff here on the loaded page
  } else {
    console.log('Ooops! Problem loading page: '
                  this.url);
    phantom.exit(1);
  }
});
```

The open method's second parameter is a callback that will be executed after the page loads, with or without an error. The function callback will have a single parameter that will hold the status of the page loading operation. The object is in the string format.

The parameter will have the value 'success' if the page is loaded, and 'fail' if there is a problem and the loading operation is not complete. In the preceding code, we have a reference to this.url, which is webpage.url; we should know that each and every property that the webpage object can be referenced as this within the function. There are several other properties that we can look into, such as frame information using frameTitle, frameUrl, framesCount, and so on. We can check out other webpage properties from the URL https://github.com/ariya/phantomjs/wiki/API-Reference-WebPage.

In the preceding example, we check if status is equal to 'success' and, if it is, then we display the appropriate message; otherwise, we will display that we have encountered a loading problem as shown in the following screenshot:

Exiting with error codes

In most cases, if we've encountered an error, we normally stop further execution of the script. It is logical to do that in most scenarios. For example, if we have a problem loading the required URL or file, we halt the process since we reference DOM objects within the page after loading; we cannot do so if the page is not available.

The PhantomJS `exit` function can accept a numeric value that will be used as the error code; it is used by calling the shell script.

```
else {
   console.log('Ooops! Problem loading page.');
   phantom.exit(1);
}
```

In the preceding code, we call the `phantom.exit` method and pass a value of `1`; this will denote our exit code that, within our script, means the page is not loaded. We can return different exit codes for different problems as we see fit.

Summary

In this chapter, we've learned how to capture different errors that PhantomJS can trigger and how to handle them. It is always a good programming practice to handle all errors in specific events practically, so that we can do more or alert our users more about the problems they might encounter. In the next chapter, we will explore PhantomJS's features to capture and save screenshots of the page we've opened. This feature can be used in a variety of ways and can also be of use in debugging the pages when errors occur by taking a snapshot of that page.

5
Grabbing Pages

Capturing the browser page as an image is very fundamental in PhantomJS; the feature was added at an early stage of the development. The basic code to take a screenshot is as follows:

```
var system = require('system');
var url = system.args[1];
var page = require('webpage').create();

page.open(url, function(status) {
  if ( status === "success" ) {
    page.render('page.png');
    phantom.exit(0);
  } else {
    phantom.exit(1);
  }
});
```

We can take a screenshot of any page using the `WebPage` object's `render()` function. It accepts a single parameter, which is the name of the file where the image is to be saved.

In the preceding code, we call the `render()` function and pass the name `page.png`, stating that we want our screenshot to be saved as a PNG file.

Upon executing it, the current state and rendered details of the page in the browser memory will be captured and saved as an image in the current folder. This will produce a PNG file that can be viewed with any image viewer. The following screenshot displays the output image of the script:

PhantomJS automatically determines the file format of the image through which the screenshot will be exported based on the file extension that we state in the filename parameter. The preceding script explicitly denotes that the name will be page.png, hence it will save and create a screenshot that is in PNG format.

The following are the three image formats that we can save to:

Format	Extension	Description
PNG	.png	Portable Network Graphics
GIF	.gif	Graphics Interchange Format
JPEG	.jpg or .jpeg	JPEG Interchange Format

If we want to save the image to another folder location, we include either the relative or the absolute path as part of the name to tell PhantomJS where to save it.

Let us slightly modify our script to the following to make it accept the file format of the screenshot to be saved to:

```
var system = require('system');
var url = system.args[1];
var saveas = system.args[2];
var page = require('webpage').create();

page.open(url, function(status) {
  if ( status === "success" ) {
    console.log('Saving screenshot as ' + saveas);
    page.render('screenshot.' + saveas);
    phantom.exit(0);
  }
});.
```

Now our script accepts two arguments; the first is the web URL and the second is the extension of the image format. We then use the extension to complete the name of our screenshot filename.

The script execution will produce a new file named page.gif. This contains the rendering of the browser page upon loading the specified URL.

Undocumented supported image format

Aside from the documented supported image formats, there are also several other formats that can be used to save the screenshot. These are as follows:

Format	Extension	Description
BMP	.bmp	Bitmap
PBM	.pbm	Portable Bitmap
PGM	.pgm	Portable Graymap
PPM	.ppm	Portable Pixmap

The following are some screenshot grabs using these formats:

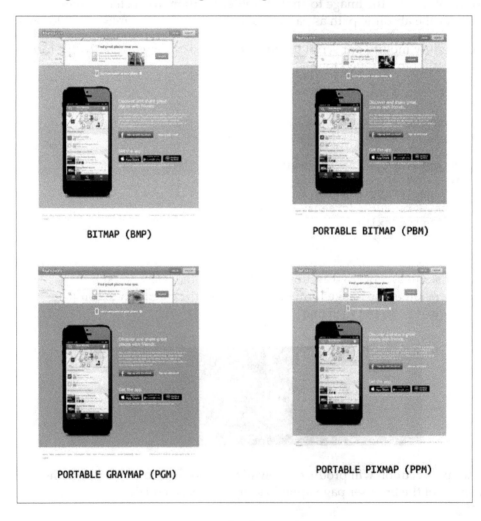

BITMAP (BMP)　　　　PORTABLE BITMAP (PBM)

PORTABLE GRAYMAP (PGM)　　　PORTABLE PIXMAP (PPM)

Although we can save in these formats, the first three file formats are more useful on the web as they are widely used in most websites that are now available.

Screenshot dimensions

PhantomJS renders the entire page depending on the size of the page or how it was supposed to be rendered in a browser. Different sites render differently. For example, if we capture a **Wikipedia** page in a normal browser, it will render something similar to the following screenshot:

The browser loads everything, but we can only see the viewable area in the browser, and we must scroll down to see everything else. In PhantomJS, it renders everything in one image. If we use our script and capture the screenshot of the preceding URL, it will give us an image with a dimension size of 777 pixels wide and 71,366 pixels long.

Having these gigantic images may cause some problems for viewing. PhantomJS allows setting the dimension size of what we have to capture. We can use the `clipRect` property of the `WebPage` object.

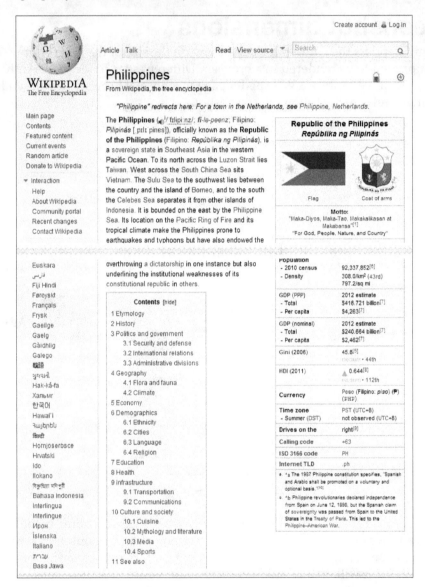

Let us say we want to limit the size of the rectangle to 800 pixels in width and 800 pixels in height. We also need to define the coordinate the clipping will start at; let's say top = 0 and left = 0. So, before we capture, we set the clipRect property to these values.

```
var system = require('system');
var url = system.args[1];
var saveas = system.args[2];
var page = require('webpage').create();

page.open(url, function(status) {
  if ( status === "success" ) {
    console.log('Saving screenshot as ' + saveas);
    page.clipRect = { top: 0, left: 0, width: 800, height: 200 };
    page.render('screenshot.' + saveas);
    phantom.exit(0);
  }
});
```

We added the settings for the clipRect property; then we called the render function. This script when used to capture our **Wikipedia** page will give the following output:

Saving web pages as PDFs

Rendering pages is not limited to images; we can also save the rendered page as a PDF document. If we state that the rendering file extension is .pdf, it will save the page as a PDF document; however, it will not automatically create multiple page documents if the page is too large. We need to set the paper properties to make a multipage PDF.

The `WebPage` object has a `paperSize` property that we can set before rendering the page to PDF. Let us say, we want to capture the page as PDF with an A4 paper size.

```
var system = require('system');
var url = system.args[1];
var saveas = system.args[2];
var page = require('webpage').create();

page.open(url, function(status) {
  if ( status === "success" ) {
    console.log('Saving screenshot as ' + saveas);
    page.paperSize = { format: 'A4',
                       orientation: 'portrait',
                       border: '1cm' };
    page.render('screenshot.' + saveas);
    phantom.exit(0);
  }
});
```

Upon setting the paper size, PhantomJS will automatically slice the page into multiple pages when captured.

Supported paper size options	
Paper format	Legal, Letter, A3, A4, A5, Tabloid
Units	mm, cm, in, px
Orientation	portrait, landscape

We can also set the custom paper sizes using the following settings:

```
page.paperSize = { width: '8in',
                   height: '11in',
                   border: '15px' };
```

Summary

Capturing screenshots is a very nifty feature of PhantomJS, and we can make a lot of useful applications with it. There are several services using this to provide the users with the capability to create varieties of screenshots of their page on different sizes; some also provide the facility of viewing and capturing pages in different hues or possible color blindness combinations. We can do a lot more using this feature, and we can actually integrate this feature using location-based services, about which we are going to learn more in the next chapter.

6
Accessing Location-based Services

Web services using location are becoming more popular. Social media sites use these to gather or display information related to the user's location. With numerous services available, we can use these services and create scripts using PhantomJS to simplify or automate some of the processes. We will discuss some of these possibilities in this chapter.

Checking a location based on IP address

IP geolocation services are widely available now and accessing them gives us new ways to look for new items on the web, such as when we want to get a list of establishments that are close to us. If we can determine the location of a user, we can customize content that is more appropriate to their location.

There are several IP geolocation services that are available and free:

Web URL	Output format
freegeoip.net	CSV, XML, and JSON
ipinfodb.com	XML
hostip.info	HTML and XML

We will use freegeoip.net since it has output in JSON and JSON is much lighter than XML or other formats; aside from this, JSON is natively supported in JavaScript. We can directly parse and manipulate JSON objects readily, without using any third-party library.

Based on the `freegeoip.net` documentation, to get the geolocation, we must use the following URL format: `http://freegeoip.net/(format)/(IP or hostname)`.

The (format) part of the URL can be one of the following: CSV, XML, or JSON. The (IP or hostname) part of the URL is optional, so we can omit that in our URL. The result in JSON for this service is as follows:

```
{
    "ip": "119.92.192.222",
    "country_code": "PH",
    "country_name": "Philippines",
    "region_code": "D9",
    "region_name": "Manila",
    "city": "Manila",
    "zipcode": "",
    "latitude": 14.6042,
    "longitude": 120.9822,
    "metro_code": "",
    "areacode": ""
}
```

 Try opening `http://freegeoip.net/json/` in a browser and it will return JSON-formatted data that corresponds to your location.

Based on this JSON data, we can open a page in the PhantomJS script; then, after successful loading, we convert the entire page content, which is in plain text, using the `page.plainText` property into JSON objects. We can now access the different properties of the JSON object, such as the IP address, city, and country name, as shown in the following code:

```
var page = require('webpage').create();
var system = require('system');

page.open('http://freegeoip.net/json/', function (status) {
  if (status == 'success') {
    var data = JSON.parse(page.plainText);
    console.log('IP Address: ' + data.ip);
    console.log('Estimated Location: ' +
                data.city + ", " + data.country_name);
  }
  phantom.exit();
});
```

In the preceding code, we open the page by passing the freegeoip JSON service URL and then, if the loading is successful, we parse the page content. We can now have different types of outputs from here since we do have access to our geolocation. Running our script will give the output shown in the following screenshot:

```
$ phantomjs getgeo.js
IP Address: 119.92.191.242
Estimated Location: Manila, Philippines

$
```

We can now use this information as input for other location-based services, such as getting directions to another point of interest or looking up certain types of establishments that are near our location.

Getting driving directions

With the vast availability of map services from Google, Bing, Yahoo!, and even MapQuest, getting directions is very easy. We will explore how to use the Google Directions API to generate driving directions from one place to another.

> First, we need the request URL of the Google Directions API. Based on the documentation, the request URL is as follows:
>
> `http://maps.googleapis.com/maps/api/directions/output?parameters`

The output can be either JSON or XML, depending on which format of output we want our result to be. We will be using JSON for our example. There are also required parameters such as those described in the following table:

Parameter	Description
origin	Beginning address
destination	Destination address
sensor	Indicator of whether or not the request is coming from a device or a location sensor; it can be either true or false

So, if we are going to get directions from Los Angeles, California to San Francisco, California, we need to use the following request URL:

```
http://maps.googleapis.com/maps/api/directions/
json?origin=Los Angeles, California&destination=San Francisco,
California&sensor=false
```

We will be setting the sensor to `false` since PhantomJS is not a device or location sensor. So, let us implement that in our script. First, we need to accept two parameters — `origin` and `destination`.

```
var page = require('webpage').create();
var system = require('system');

var origin = system.args[1];
var destination = system.args[2];
```

Then, we open a new page using our request URL, but instead of hardcoding the origin and destination, we will be dynamically adding our parameters to our URL.

```
page.open(encodeURI('http://maps.googleapis.com/maps/'
                + 'api/directions/json'
                + '?origin=' + origin
                + '&destination=' + destination
                + '&sensor=false'), function (status) {
    if (status === 'success') {
```

If we successfully load our page, we can parse and convert the page content into a JSON object.

```
var direction = JSON.parse(page.plainText);
```

Our next step is to traverse the JSON object and get directions. But, before we can do that, we must know the structure of the Google Direction API JSON result, as shown in the following screenshot:

```
status (string)
routes (array)

    legs (array)
        start_address (string)
        end_address (string)
        steps (array)
            {
                html_instruction (string)
                travel_mode (string)
                duration (object)
                    text (string)
                    value (string)
                distance (object)
                    text (string)
                    value (string)
            }
```

The preceding screenshot is the JSON result structure of the Google Direction API. It is just a subset of the structure of the result data and this will be enough for our example. You can get the complete JSON format in the Google Direction API documentation of the JSON result at https://developers.google.com/maps/documentation/directions/#JSON

We can get the status of the request using the status property and, if we get the status of OK, the direction is available for us to parse.

```
if(direction.status == 'OK'){
```

The result may contain multiple routes and each route may have multiple legs of direction. We will only get the first route and the first leg. Based on the result, we first get the starting address. This may contain the full address. We get that using the start_address property (see the following line of code):

```
console.log("A - " +
           direction.routes[0].legs[0].start_address);
```

Next, we traverse each step under the first leg of the result. We extract the steps property array and then loop for each item.

```
var steps = direction.routes[0].legs[0].steps;
var step_ctr = 0;
steps.forEach(function (step) {
  step_ctr++;
  var instruction =
    step.html_instructions.replace(/(<([^>]+)>)/ig, "");
  console.log(step_ctr + " - " + instruction);
});
```

The directions can be found in the html_instructions property of each step, so we output that as part of our step-by-step direction instructions. As per the property name html_instructions, this property contains HTML tags that Google intends to be visualized in a browser. We can remove all the HTML tags within the html_instructions value using a simple replace action.

Within this loop, we can add more details, such as the distance for this step and the estimated duration. Lastly, to complete our direction instructions, we output the end address or the destination.

```
console.log("B - " + direction.routes[0].legs[0].end_address);
```

We can also add something like checking whether or not the status of the result is OK to determine whether or not to display an error message. Let's execute our script as follows:

```
sources — bash — 120×14

$ phantomjs getdirection.js "Los Angeles, California" "San Francisco, California"
A - Los Angeles, CA, USA
1 - Head northwest on W 1st St toward S Spring St
2 - Turn right at the 2nd cross street onto N Broadway
3 - Turn right to merge onto Hwy 101 N/US-101 N toward I-110 N
4 - Keep left to continue on CA-170 N/Hollywood Fwy, follow signs for Sacramento
5 - Keep left at the fork, follow signs for Interstate 5 N/Sacramento and merge onto I-5 N
6 - Keep left to continue on I-580 W, follow signs for Tracy/San Francisco
7 - Keep right to stay on I-580 W, follow signs for Oakland/San Francisco
8 - Take the exit on the left onto I-80 W toward San FranciscoPartial toll road
9 - Keep right at the fork, follow signs for U.S. 101 N/Golden Gate Bridge and merge onto Hwy 101 N/US-101 N
10 - Turn right onto Market St
B - San Francisco, CA, USA

$
```

You can get more information about the Google Direction API in the following URL:

`https://developers.google.com/maps/documentation/directions/`

Looking up for pizza delivery establishments

With these location-based services, not only can we get directions, but we can also look up establishments that are within our area. There are several services that are available for looking up restaurants, stores, and food delivery establishments; some of these include **Yelp** and **Yahoo Local Search**.

In our example, we will use the Yahoo Local Search API, which also has support for returning results in the JSON format. We will also follow the same technique as we did for getting directions. We must refer to the Yahoo Local Search Web Services API for the parameters and format of the URL request. You can check out the documentation in the following URL:

`http://developer.yahoo.com/search/local/V3/localSearch.html`

Based on the documentation, we need to pass the following parameters to successfully get a result:

Parameter	Description	Value
appid	This is the application ID. You can register to get your own at http://developer.yahoo.com/wsregapp/	YahooDemo (for demo purposes only)
query	This is the string used for searching.	For example: Pizza, Car, and Cinema
location/zip	This is the address where the requester is located. Yahoo Local Search only works in the US.	Los Angeles, CA
output	XML, JSON, or PHP.	By default, it outputs as XML

With this information, let us create our local search script and look for pizza delivery establishments. Our script will accept two arguments, query or search string, and our address.

```
var page = require('webpage').create();
var system = require('system');

var query = system.args[1];
var address = system.args[2];
```

Then, we open a new page using our request URL and dynamically add our parameters.

```
page.open(encodeURI('http://local.yahooapis.com/LocalSearchService
                    /V3/localSearch'
            + '?appid=YahooDemo'
            + '&query=' + query
            + '&location=' + address
            + '&results=2&output=json'), function (status) {
    if (status == 'success') {
```

After we successfully retrieve the result, we can parse and traverse the list. Please refer to Yahoo!'s documentation regarding the output format for complete reference. We will only use some of the data as part of our script, such as the address, business URL, or phone number, as shown in the following code:

```
var localsearch = JSON.parse(page.plainText);
if(localsearch.ResultSet.totalResultsAvailable == '0'){
```

```
        console.log('No result found.');
    } else {
        console.log("Top results are:");
        var results = localsearch.ResultSet.Result;
        results.forEach(function (result) {
            console.log(result.Title);
            console.log(result.Address + ", "
                    + result.City + ", "
                    + result.State);
            console.log(result.Phone);
            console.log(result.BusinessUrl);
            console.log("Ratings : " + result.Rating.AverageRating);
            console.log("");
        });
    }
```

We can determine whether or not the query found is something related to our query. In the preceding code; we can check the total results available. If we have a result, we can iterate each item in the result property, as shown in the following screenshot:

Summary

Location-based services are a very useful capability and, from what we've learned in this chapter, we can create our very own service by integrating the three examples we've featured. We can create search or directory services that allow users to find establishments and give them easy access to directions to get there from their location that we can also retrieve using the geolocation example. In the next chapter, we will understand how PhantomJS allows us to read and write files using its own FileSystem API.

7
Working with Files

Reading and writing to files are some of the basic tasks in programming. These functions are commonly used in reading and saving the configuration of the application, persisting important data, or for logging application activities. PhantomJS provides a rich FileSystem API that supports most of the file handling and operations needed. The API contains similar functions that can be found in other programming language. In this chapter we will cover the checking, loading, and writing of files using PhantomJS's built-in file handling capabilities.

PhantomJS FileSystem API

The FileSystem module of PhantomJS provides mechanisms to manipulate files, folders, paths, and contents. It is also capable of handling file object streams. The API is handy and very easy to use.

Let us start with a very simple example, using the API to display the folder we are working on.

```
var fs = require('fs');
console.log("Working Directory: " + fs.workingDirectory);
phantom.exit(0);
```

In the first line, we reference an instance of the FileSystem module using the `require` keyword and passing `fs` as the module name. With this, we can now access all the file and folder functions.

```
$ phantomjs file1.js
Working Directory: /book/chapter7/sources

$
```

Reading files

There are various reasons as to why we need to read a file within our script; for most examples, we may need to read a configuration file that is relatively needed in our script execution. Let us learn how to read files using the API.

Checking for file existence

Before we actually read the file content, it is better to check the file's existence so that we can prevent possible file reading errors. Using the API, we can check if the file exists using the `exists` function.

```
fs.exists('/data/myfiles/config.txt')
```

However, this function does not guarantee that the file we are checking is a true file; it may be a directory. The path that can be passed onto the function might be a folder path, which also returns `true` if the folder path is correct and if it does exist. So, to make it more accurate, we can also combine the testing of the file's existence using the `isFile` function. This function also accepts the file path as a parameter and returns `true` if the path is a file (and not a directory).

```
var filePath = '/book/chapter7/sources/file1.js';
if( fs.exists(filePath) && fs.isFile(filePath) ) {
```

With this function, rest assured that the file exists when we opened the file for reading.

Opening the file

Now, we can open the file for reading using the `open(path, mode)` function. The `mode` parameter can be any one of the following values:

File open mode	Functions
r	Open file for reading
w	File mode is set for writing
a	Append mode
rb	Reading binary files
wb	Writing binary files

We will now use the `open` function to read a text file; see the following code:

```
var ins = fs.open(filePath, 'r');
```

If the file is opened successfully, it will return an object of the `stream` type. This object has the capability to manipulate the content of the opened file either for reading or writing.

```
var ins = fs.open(filePath, 'r');
console.log(ins.read());
```

In the preceding lines of code, we use the object stream and issue the `read()` function. This will read all the content of the file and return it to the method. We can stream that data as we like, or simply print it to the console.

Let us modify the preceding little code and make it more functional. For example, our script will need to read a file that contains some configuration details, and this file is in JSON format, as follows:

```
{
    "home": "/phantomjs/src",
    "debug": false
}
```

As we now know, we can actually read its entire contents just by using the `read()` function, and with that, it will return the content of the file. Using JavaScript JSON parsing, we can convert the text into a functional JSON object.

```
var ins = fs.open(filePath, 'r');
var data = ins.read();
var config = JSON.parse(data);
console.log("Home: " + config.home);
```

Alternatively, in the preceding lines of code, we can combine the first three lines into one line as follows:

```
var config = JSON.parse(fs.open(filePath, 'r').read());
```

If we run our code, it should display that the home directory is /phantomjs/src, which comes from the file that was read:

```
sources — bash — 120×14
$ phantomjs file4.js json.txt
Home: /phantomjs/src
$
```

Alternatively, we can also read the file line by line. In some cases, this will be necessary, especially when we are processing each line separately when parsing a CSV file. We can do this by using the readLine() function instead. On every function call, the readLine() function will return one line of string from the file. We can parse each line by using the split() function to tokenize the string.

```
var ins = fs.open(filePath, 'r');
while(!ins.atEnd()) {
  var buffer = ins.readLine();
  site = buffer.split(/\s*,\s*/);

  console.log(site[0]);
  console.log('--------------------------');
  console.log('Web: ' + site[1]);
  console.log('Since: ' + site[2] + '\n');
}
```

If we are reading the file line by line, then we need to check whether we have reached the end of the file. We can do this by using the atEnd() function of the stream object. This function will return true if we reach the end of the file; otherwise, it will return false.

If we have the following CSV content:

```
Facebook,www.facebook.com,2004
Foursquare,www.foursquare.com,2009
Google+,plus.google.com,2011
```

And we execute our script against that CSV content, then we will have the following output:

```
$ phantomjs file3.js
Facebook
--------------------------
Web: www.facebook.com
Since: 2004

Foursquare
--------------------------
Web: www.foursquare.com
Since: 2009

Google+
--------------------------
Web: plus.google.com
Since: 2011
$
```

Closing the opened files

Our last step after reading the content of the file is to close the stream. Calling the `close()` function from the `stream` object will mark the file stream as closed and no more operations can be called against it.

```
ins.close();
```

Writing files

There are several modes in opening a file, and so far, we have only used the `read(r)` mode. To open a file for writing, we can use the following syntax:

```
var ins = fs.open(filePath, 'w');
```

This will create a new `stream` object that we can use to write new content to. For example, in our script we have a configuration that is in JSON object format. Let us assume that the configuration object can be changed during runtime and we need that state to be saved back to configuration. Let's say we need to save some new values to our configuration file.

```
var config = {
  debug: true,
  home: '/home/phantomjs',
  username: 'tarab'
};
```

```
var out = fs.open(filePath, 'w');
// File opened for writing
out.write(JSON.stringify(config, null, 4));
out.close();

phantom.exit(0);
```

After opening the file for writing, we use the `write` function and pass the string value of the JSON object to be written to the file. With this simple function call we have written a simple content to a file.

Just as we saw while reading file contents, we can also write data to files line-per-line using the `writeLine()` function. This approach can be very useful while writing processed data one line at a time.

Character encoding

In some cases, we need to specify the character encoding of the file we are creating or reading to ensure that data being processed is in the correct format. In the PhantomJS FileSystem API, these file character encodings are supported, but undocumented. These encodings can be defined while opening the files for reading and writing. We can do this by specifying multiple attributes in the file's `mode` parameter.

```
var out = fs.open(filePath, {mode: 'w', charset: 'UTF-8'});
```

Reading and writing functions will be the same even with a defined character encoding, which is specific to the file.

The FileSystem API not only supports reading and writing of files, but also contains functions that allow you to traverse folder structures, delete, move, and rename files and folders.

Summary

What we have learned in this chapter can be very useful in most of the applications developed using PhantomJS. More often than not, we will be creating applications to read and write configuration files that are essential to the inner workings of our applications. For implementing these, the FileSystem API can help us greatly. We can also do simple message logging by writing some debug information to a file, to help out in debugging and program tracing. In the next chapter we will learn more about how PhantomJS supports cookies, and how we can use them in our application.

8
Cookies

Cookies are mostly used to save small information about users' activities during visits on a particular site. Most often, this information is used when the user visits the site again, like knowing which particular search the user used or the page from where the user left off. PhantomJS supports cookies and has a minimal API to manage cookies within the `phantom` object.

Default cookies are enabled in PhantomJS, and we can also disable cookies by setting the following property:

```
phantom.cookiesEnabled = false;
```

Reading cookies

Each cookie that a web page generates or creates will be stored in the `phantom.cookies` object.

To retrieve all the cookies, we access the `cookies` member. Let us print the `cookies` object:

```
page.open(url, function(status) {
  if ( status === "success" ) {
    console.log(phantom.cookies);
    phantom.exit(0);
  }
});
```

If there are cookies in the website that we are accessing, then you should see output similar to the following screenshot:

```
                              sources — bash — 120×14
$ phantomjs cookies1.js http://www.yahoo.com
[object Object],[object Object],[object Object],[object Object],[object Object],[object Object],[object Object],
[object Object],[object Object],[object Object],[object Object],[object Object],[object Object],[object Object],
[object Object],[object Object],[object Object]

$
```

Based on the preceding output, .yahoo.com has several cookies. These cookies vary on the website or URL. Each cookie is in object form, which can be viewed as a JSON object. Each cookie object will have the following properties:

```
{
    'name'     : 'name of cookie',
    'value'    : 'value associated',
    'domain'   : 'cookie domain',
    'path'     : 'cookie path',
    'httponly' : (true or false),
    'secure'   : (true or false),
    'expires'  : integer value of cookie expiration in seconds
}
```

If we change a bit of our code, we can make the cookies readable by converting the JSON object into a string version using the following code:

```
console.log(JSON.stringify(phantom.cookies, null, 4));
```

Then, we will have a more readable output, as shown in the following screenshot:

```
$ phantomjs cookies2.js http://www.yahoo.com
[
    {
        "domain": ".overture.com",
        "expires": "Thu, 20 Apr 2023 03:31:50 GMT",
        "expiry": 1681961510,
        "httponly": false,
        "name": "UserData",
        "path": "/",
        "secure": false,
        "value": "02u3hs9yoaLQsFTjBpMnY2N3U0NHN0cnZ2cjNTdk%2bLSi4sTU1JNbEBAGNDI1dnNyNnFzcASzlaVg0="
    },
    {
        "domain": ".overture.com",
        "expires": "Thu, 23 Apr 2015 20:00:00 GMT",
        "expiry": 1429819200,
        "httponly": false,
        "name": "BX",
        "path": "/",
        "secure": false,
```

Baking some cookies

How about creating our own cookies? Normally, users do not push the creation of cookies, but in PhantomJS, we can do that in our script to change the browser behavior.

Let us modify our previous code, and before displaying the list of cookies, we will add a `"username"` property to the cookie.

```javascript
page.open(url, function(status) {
    if ( status === "success" ) {
        phantom.addCookie({
            'name'   : 'username',
            'value'  : 'aries',
            'domain' : '.yahoo.com'
        });
        console.log(JSON.stringify(phantom.cookies, null, 4));
        phantom.exit(0);
    }
});
```

We will use the `addCookie` function from the `phantom` object. The function expects an object to be passed in JSON format. However, the `name`, `value`, and `domain` property are the only properties required to be present; all other properties are optional.

Cookie property	Expected value
name	The name of the cookie must be present. As per cookie specification, a cookie name must not start with $, which is reserved.
value	This is the value of the cookie; it is required.
domain	The domain name that this cookie is valid is required. The domain must start with a dot.
path	The path of the document that this cookie is applied. This defaults to the current path if not specified.
httponly	`true` or `false`, states that when set to `true`, the value of the cookie should be used only with HTTP, and that any other client side should prevent access to this cookie. For more information about this property, we can check out the HttpOnly working group site: `http://groups.google.com/group/ietf-httponly-wg`
secure	`true` or `false`, states that if the cookie is valid in secured connection, then this should be `true`.
expires	Time in milliseconds.

If we run this script, the newly added cookie will be on top and will be displayed first from the list.

We can add as much as we can, but technically, a cookie must not be more than 255 characters long and can only consume up to 4 KB of disk space.

Deleting cookies

In the previous section, we created a new cookie for the `yahoo.com` domain with the name `'username'`. We can also delete the same cookie simply by passing its name to the `deleteCookie` function:

```
if( phantom.deleteCookie('username') ) {
  console.log('Cookie deleted.');
} else {
  console.log('Cookie not deleted or does not exist.');
}
```

If the desired cookie is not present, the function will not generate any error, but it will return a `false` value. To clear all cookies, simply use the `clearCookies` function.

```
phantom.clearCookies();
```

Keeping cookies

In PhantomJS, cookies are not persistent by default. All cookies and cookie manipulation in our script will be destroyed and gone after the script execution. Each time we call our script, it will recreate the cookies again as if we had not visited the page before. If we need to persist with our cookies (like browsers do), we need to specify a cookie file. This cookie file will save all cookies from the different sites and domains we visit into a text file. The cookie file is passed in via the PhantomJS command line:

```
phantomjs –cookies-file=~/phantomjs/cookies.txt cookies1.js
```

If the cookie file does not exist yet, PhantomJS will create one; if it does exist, then it will load the cookies from the file we specified.

Summary

Cookies are very useful in some web applications. They are most commonly used to track user activity or choice while using the application. We can also create more test scenarios based on cookies. This will depend on how cookies are used in web applications. PhantomJS provides a trivial API for cookie handling, but it does the job for most cases.

9
External JavaScript

In most development projects, it is essential to organize our code into separate files or modules to facilitate readability and reuse. PhantomJS supports a module-loading mechanism that allows us to load and use external JavaScript. It uses the CommonJS API standard (`http://wiki.commonjs.org`).

Modules

In earlier chapters, we discussed PhantomJS's built-in modules. Let us explore how to create our own modules and use them in our PhantomJS scripts.

First, let's create a straightforward module of a timer that can measure the duration of a given process based on calling the `start` and `stop` functions. Let us define the variables to be used. We will require `timeStart`, `timeStop`, and a `duration` variable to hold the duration when the `stop` function is called.

In a normal JavaScript, we will define our variable as the following:

```
var timeStart = null;
```

However, for our modules, we need to use the `exports` keyword to indicate that the variables belong to the external module, so let us change our previous code to the following:

```
exports.timeStart = null;
exports.timeStop = null;
exports.duration = 0;
```

These variables are now available in our module. We can now use them within our scripts. We can access them and set new values or display the current data. Let us do this before proceeding. We save our module and name it `"timer.js"`. We now call our module `timer`. To use this module in our script, we will use the `require` keyword to load it. Note that the `.js` extension is optional.

```
var timer = require("./timer");
```

We can use a relative path to load our module as we did in the preceding line of code. If we have this main script on the same path as `timer.js`, then our module will be loaded. Please note that we need to specify our own module using a relative path or top-level script. Unless we specify all of this, PhantomJS will try to load the module as its own predefined module.

Now, let's add more calls in our main script to access some timer-defined variables or member fields.

```
var timer = require("./timer");
console.log(timer.duration);
```

Let us save this script as `main.js` and then execute it.

In the second line of the preceding code, we are able to access our module member field `duration`, and we are able to retrieve and print the current value of `0`. Let us complete our module and add some useful functions to complete our `timer` module with the help of the following code:

```
exports.timeStart = null;
exports.timeStop = null;
exports.duration = 0;
exports.start = function() {
  this.timeStart = new Date();
};
exports.stop = function() {
  this.timeStop = new Date();
  this.duration = this.timeStop - this.timeStart;
};
```

Now that we have our custom module, let us digest our code. After the variable declaration, we defined the first function that will record the start of our timer. This function is also prefixed with the keyword `exports`, which exposes it to the code that requires our module. The function logic is just like that of any other JavaScript function. However, since we are going to reference any variable or function that is defined in our module, we will reference them with the `this` keyword to denote that we are accessing artifacts that belong in our module.

Now, we can make use of this module. Say we want to measure how long it takes to load a particular URL. We begin by creating typical boilerplate code to define the `webpage` and `system` modules for the arguments and finally get the first argument of the script as the URL to be loaded.

```
var system = require('system');
var page = require("webpage").create();
var timer = require("./timer");

var url = system.args[1];
```

We also load our `timer` module as seen in the third line of the preceding code. After getting the URL, we start our timer and state that we are loading a URL.

```
timer.start();
console.log("Loading " + url);
```

We called our function `start` in the first line of the preceding code, which is defined in the `timer` module, and based on our code, it saves the current time as the start time that will be used to compute the duration when the `stop` function is called.

```
page.open(url, function(status) {
    timer.stop();
    console.log("Duration: "
                + (timer.duration/1000)
                + " secs");
    phantom.exit(0);
});
```

In the first line of the preceding code, we load the web page. As we have learned, we can define a function that will be called after the loading of the page is done. Our anonymous callback is called when loading is completed, and we now call our timer `stop` function on the second line. This function saves the current time as our end time, and using the start time, this function also computes the actual duration and saves that in our `duration` variable.

We then display the computed duration in the third line of the preceding code by accessing the `duration` variable of our `timer` module. Executing our code will output the following:

```
sources — bash — 120×14
$ phantomjs main.js http://www.twitter.com
Loading http://www.twitter.com
Duration: 2.092 secs

$
```

Using the object-oriented modules

What if we want to use our module as an object with a specific type similar to a class? We can also do this with PhantomJS. Instead of using `exports`, we use `module.exports`. So what is the difference between the two? Exports are like a typical module instance that can be directly accessed like an instantiated object, but the latter is a blueprint or class that we can instantiate, and has a specific object type and properties.

 Learn more about CommonJS and its concepts by checking out the CommonJS wiki page at `http://wiki.commonjs.org/`.

So how do we create `module.exports`? Let's try one example and build it up as we progress.

First, we create our module. Let's model a person as our object and name our module as `person.js`.

```
module.exports = function() {
};
```

The code above represents a module, although it doesn't give any value. Instead of using `exports`, we define our function with `module.exports`. Actually, the function definition is our object constructor. So if we are going to use this in our implementation script, we will use it like this. Create a new implementation script, name it `main2.js`, and have the following as script code:

```
var Person = require("./person");
var tara = new Person();
```

In the first line of the preceding code, we load our module and assign the loaded module as `Person`. Using this object type, we can create an object instance as demonstrated in the second line.

That was easy! Let us move on and put some valuable code in our `person` module. We will modify our constructor and add two parameters: the name of the person and the birthdate in JavaScript's `Date` format.

```
module.exports = function(name, bday) {
  this.name = name;
  this.bday = bday;
};
```

In the first line of the preceding code, our function accepts the name and birthday parameters when creating an instance. In the second and third line, we assign the passed parameters to our member variables. We define our member variables and reference them using the `this` keyword; it is almost the same as what we have previously discussed. Updating our implementation script should result in the following:

```
var Person = require("./person");
var tara = new Person("Tara", new Date(2003, 0, 23));
console.log(tara.name);
phantom.exit(0);
```

Now, we update our constructor and pass `Tara` as name and her birthday. And by accessing the `name` variable, we get the name that we passed in the constructor since we assigned it to a member variable of our object type.

How about methods? Let us add a method to our object that returns the age of the person using the birthday that was passed in the constructor.

```
module.exports = function(name, bday) {
  this.name = name;
  this.bday = bday;

  this.getAge = function() {
    var today = new Date();
    return today.getYear() - this.bday.getYear();
  };
};
```

From the fifth line to the eighth line, we define the `getAge` method. Basically, the function computes the person's age using the birthday and the current date.

```
var Person = require("./person");
var tara = new Person("Tara", new Date(2003, 0, 23));
console.log(tara.name + " is now "
        + tara.getAge() + " years old");
```

With the instantiated object, we can call the object function, and it should return the age of the person.

```
$ phantomjs main2.js
Tara is now 10 years old

$
```

Using third-party JavaScript libraries

JavaScript libraries are widely available and can make our coding much easier rather than starting from nothing. PhantomJS supports standard JavaScript, and making use of these libraries is supported. There are two ways to inject external JavaScript into PhantomJS: by using either the `phantom` object or the `webpage` module.

When external JavaScript is loaded within the `phantom` object, we can access the external script within our script globally. When JavaScript is injected within the `webpage` object, we can use these libraries with the page document to manipulate or extract data from the loaded page. Regardless of the loading method, the use of these scripts is dependent on how well they are coded and their purpose. For example, injecting jQuery is very useful for manipulating DOM elements.

```
var page = require('webpage').create();
page.open("https://github.com/", function(status) {
  if ( status === "success" ) {
    page.render("before.png");
    page.includeJs("http://code.jquery.com/jquery-1.10.1.min.js",
    function() {
      page.evaluate(function() {
        $('.heading').html('PhantomJS');
      });
      page.render("after.png");
      phantom.exit();();
    });
  }
});
```

In the preceding code, we dynamically include the jQuery JavaScript Library using `includeJs` function of the `webpage` module. jQuery can be accessing within the page, and using jQuery in the eighth line, denotes that we are replacing a particular DOM element with a new text of `PhantomJS`.

Running our code will generate two screenshots of the page: the first screenshot is before modification of the DOM element, and the second is taken after replacing the text on that element.

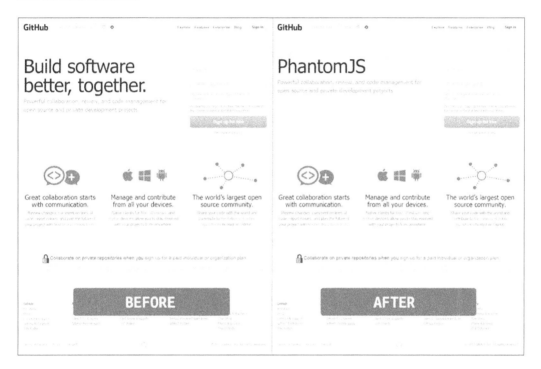

Summary

There are tons of JavaScript libraries that are useful for manipulating the page content, and some are utilities that are very handy for coding with JavaScript. This feature of loading using third-party libraries with PhantomJS can make it easier for us to code scripts. We should also start building our own libraries using PhantomJS modules that we learned earlier in this chapter. In the next chapter, we will explore the use of testing with PhantomJS, and we will also learn one of the popular JavaScript testing frameworks: Jasmine.

10
Testing with PhantomJS

Writing unit and automated tests is a critical part of the development process. Unit tests will save us a lot of time when making big changes to our code. They will also prevent regression and catch bugs earlier on. Using PhantomJS, we will discuss unit testing in this chapter and learn how we can maximize the use of PhantomJS for creating these tests.

What is unit testing?

Unit testing is the practice of testing a smaller unit of code, which can be a function or area of code that we can isolate. This gives us the ability to determine if the function behaves as expected. These tests are independent of each other and can be executed individually. Each can verify for outputs based on the given inputs, determine if the process will cause errors, and also check if the process can handle exceptions. Using unit testing, we can catch code problems and trace them easily. There are more benefits of using unit testing, and it is probably one of the necessities in programming. To learn more about unit testing, visit the following URL:

```
https://en.wikipedia.org/wiki/Unit_testing
```

Unit testing with Jasmine

Let's first explore how we can use PhantomJS to run unit tests using **Jasmine**, JavaScript's testing framework (`http://pivotal.github.io/jasmine/`). There are several testing frameworks for JavaScript that are freely available to use. Some of the better known testing frameworks are Jasmine, **QUnit**, and **Mocha**. Why Jasmine? Jasmine is also one of the more popular testing frameworks.

Besides, Jasmine syntaxes are very much like the English language when used, making it easy to follow and read the content of the test, just like in a document. In this chapter, we will not discuss Jasmine in depth, but only concentrate on those parts that we will need in our code. For more information on how to use the Jasmine API, refer to the Jasmine project page at `http://pivotal.github.io/jasmine/`.

We will assume that you know about unit testing and are familiar with it. Let's start by creating a simple calculator in JavaScript that has the ability to perform addition, subtraction, multiplication, and division. We'll name our script as `Calculator.js` and save it in the `src` folder.

```javascript
function Calculator() {
  this.currentTotal = 0;
}

Calculator.prototype.set = function(newValue) {
  this.currentTotal = newValue;
  return this.currentTotal;
};

Calculator.prototype.add = function(toAdd) {
  this.currentTotal += toAdd;
  return this.currentTotal;
};

Calculator.prototype.subtract = function(toSub) {
  this.currentTotal -= toSub;
  return this.currentTotal;
};

Calculator.prototype.divide = function(toDivide) {
  if (toDivide === 0) {
    throw "Error division by zero";
  }
  this.currentTotal /= toDivide;
  return this.currentTotal;
};
```

This is our simple calculator code that will handle basic calculation. Let's take a closer look at some parts of the code and start with the addition block. In the preceding code, we define the `add` function; it accepts a parameter that is to be added to the current total value. In the following line, we just coded an expression that performs the addition of the `toAdd` variable, which holds the value to be added to `currentTotal`. This is a very simple function and can be tested easily.

Downloading Jasmine

So, let's use Jasmine to create a test for our simple code, but before we do that, let's first download Jasmine. We can go to the previously mentioned URL, or use the URL `https://github.com/pivotal/jasmine/downloads` and download the stable, standalone version. Upon download, we will extract the files to any working directory that we can use; it is recommended that we create a `jasmine` folder and extract it there.

From the extracted package, there are a few important files and folders that we need to be familiar with. They are as follows:

`lib`	The `lib` folder contains the main Jasmine library that we need.
`spec`	The `spec` folder contains sample Jasmine test code; you'll see tests often referred to as specs because they contain mini-specifications for how a piece of code should behave.
`src`	The `src` folder contains sample code that is being tested by the specs.
`SpecRunner.html`	Spec runners such as Jasmine Spec Runner import code to be tested and enable the spec to run the test against the code. If we load this in a browser, we will be able to see whether our test passed or failed. This can act as a template when using Jasmine Spec Runner.

Test specs with Jasmine

Before we start coding Jasmine test specs, we need to be familiar with several Jasmine functions; these include `describe()`, `it()`, `expect()`, and matchers.

The `describe()` function is our test suite, and it requires two parameters to be passed onto it: the name of our test suite and the function block that holds the test specs.

```
describe("Calculator", function() {

});
```

The function block is where we will define our test specs using the `it()` function. The first parameter of the `it()` function can be any descriptive text through which we can define our test.

```
it("should able to add positive numbers", function() {
  calc.set(0);
  expect(calc.add(1)).toEqual(1);
  expect(calc.add(3)).toEqual(4);
});
```

Each block will be our test case where we can put in scripts that perform the functionalities of our application, and that may contain one or more expectations. Expectations are used in the function block with the built-in `expect()` function, which takes the actual value coming from the application. Each expect call is matched with matchers that perform equality comparisons against the actual value, as described in `expect()`, and the value is passed as the expected value of the test. There are several matchers that are available, such as `toEqual()`, `toBe()`, `toContain()`, and `toBeNull()`. We need to read more about each matcher from the Jasmine documentation (`http://pivotal.github.io/jasmine/#section-Matchers`). Let us move on and create a complete test spec that we will use to test our mini-calculator application.

```
describe("Calculator", function() {
  var calc;

  beforeEach(function() {
    calc = new Calculator();
  });

  it("should be able to add positive numbers", function() {
    calc.set(0);
    nexpect(calc.add(1)).toEqual(1);
    expect(calc.add(3)).toEqual(4);
    expect(calc.add(2)).toEqual(6);
    expect(calc.add(4)).toEqual(10);
  });

  it("should be able to add negative numbers", function() {
    calc.set(10);
    expect(calc.add(-1)).toEqual(9);
    expect(calc.add(-4)).toEqual(5);
  });

  it("should be able to subtract positive numbers", function() {
    calc.set(10);
    expect(calc.subtract(1)).toEqual(9);
    expect(calc.subtract(3)).toEqual(6);
    expect(calc.subtract(2)).toEqual(4);
    expect(calc.subtract(4)).toEqual(0);
  });
```

```
  it("should be able to subtract negative numbers", function() {
    calc.set(10);
    expect(calc.subtract(-1)).toEqual(11);
    expect(calc.subtract(-3)).toEqual(14);
    expect(calc.subtract(-2)).toEqual(16);
    expect(calc.subtract(-4)).toEqual(20);
  });
});
```

The preceding code is a Jasmine test suite code that contains describe() and several it() specs with different expectations. We also have a new block in the specs, which define a beforeEach() function. This function will be called for each test before the function block of each it() block is performed. So in that line, the calculator object will be reinstantiated for each test case. Let us save our code as CalculatorSpec.js inside the test folder. We'll have to create the test folder if we don't have one.

To complete our test code, we will modify the Jasmine Spec Runner example and make it our own. Let us take a look at the SpecRunner.html example and apply our change to it later on.

```
<!DOCTYPE HTML PUBLIC "-//W3C//DTD HTML 4.01 Transitional//EN"
  "http://www.w3.org/TR/html4/loose.dtd">

<html>
  <head>
    <title>Jasmine Spec Runner</title>
    <link rel="shortcut icon" type="image/png"
      href="lib/jasmine-1.3.1/jasmine_favicon.png">
    <link rel="stylesheet" type="text/css"
      href="lib/jasmine-1.3.1/jasmine.css">
    <script type="text/javascript"
      src="lib/jasmine-1.3.1/jasmine.js"></script>
    <script type="text/javascript"
      src="lib/jasmine-1.3.1/jasmine-html.js"></script>
    <!-- include source files here... -->
    <script type="text/javascript"
      src="src/Player.js"></script>
    <script type="text/javascript" src="src/Song.js"></script>
    <!-- include spec files here... -->
    <script type="text/javascript"
      src="spec/SpecHelper.js"></script>
    <script type="text/javascript"
      src="spec/PlayerSpec.js"></script>
    <script type="text/javascript">
```

```
(function() {
  var jasmineEnv = jasmine.getEnv();
  jasmineEnv.updateInterval = 1000;
  var htmlReporter = new jasmine.HtmlReporter();
  jasmineEnv.addReporter(htmlReporter);
  jasmineEnv.specFilter = function(spec) {
    return htmlReporter.specFilter(spec);
  };
  var currentWindowOnload = window.onload;
  window.onload = function() {
    if (currentWindowOnload) {
      currentWindowOnload();
    }
    execJasmine();
  };
  function execJasmine() {
    jasmineEnv.execute();
  }
})();
    </script>
  </head>
  <body>
  </body>
</html>
```

The preceding code is an example from Jasmine's distribution package. This spec runner will be our template for running our own little test specs. From the preceding code, we replace the included JavaScript files with our own calculator application. We will replace the `Player` and `Song` JavaScript files with the following:

```
<!-- include source files here... -->
<script type="text/javascript"
  src="src/Calculator.js"></script>
```

The preceding code snippet will load our calculator application, and to make it complete, we will need to include our test spec in it. The example test spec is defined, and we will replace that with our `CalculatorSpec.js` file.

```
<!-- include spec files here... -->
<script type="text/javascript"
  src="test/CalculatorSpec.js"></script>
```

After modifying the two sections, we will leave everything else. We do not need to touch any other part of the `SpecRunner.html` file.

 In order to run Jasmine specs, load the `SpecRunner.html` file in your browser.

Running the test spec in our browser will produce the following screenshot:

```
Jasmine 1.3.1 revision 1354556913                          finished in 0.013s

• • • •

Passing 4 specs                                            No try/catch ■

Calculator
   should able to add positive numbers
   should able to add negative numbers
   should able to subtract positive numbers
   should able to subtract negative numbers
```

The preceding screenshot shows that our test passes for all the test cases. If there are failed test items, they will also be shown in the result page. Let's add a new test that will fail when we add a new test case for an unimplemented feature.

Our calculator does not support the multiplication of numbers yet, but we do want to add this feature. To do this, we first need to add our test specs for multiplication before implementing the multiplication code itself. So, we need to create another `it()` block for the multiplication test spec in our `CalculatorSpec.js` file as follows:

```
it("should be able to multiply numbers", function() {
  calc.set(10);
  expect(calc.multiply(1)).toEqual(10);
  expect(calc.multiply(2)).toEqual(20);
  expect(calc.multiply(3)).toEqual(60);
  expect(calc.multiply(4)).toEqual(240);
});
```

Running our spec runner should show that there are failed tests, as shown in the following screenshot:

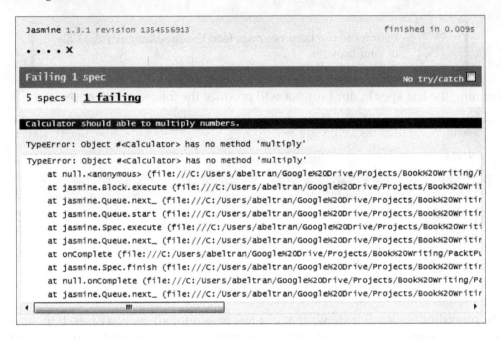

Since we don't have that function yet, our test will fail and tell us that there are no methods with `multiply` from our calculator object. So, let's make this test pass by implementing the multiplication feature.

Let's edit our `Calculator.js` script and add the following block of code:

```
Calculator.prototype.multiply = function(toMultiply) {
  this.currentTotal *= toMultiply;
  return this.currentTotal;
};
```

Without modifying anything else, running our test runner should produce an all-passed test suite.

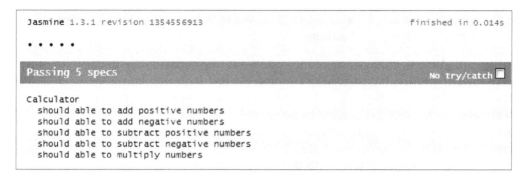

If there are problems or bugs in our implementation code, our test will produce a failed test run and Jasmine will highlight which of the test specs has the problem.

The PhantomJS Jasmine runner

From this point on, we will move to PhantomJS and see how we are going to use it to run Jasmine test specs. What we have learned about Jasmine is enough for us to move forward and learn how to use it with PhantomJS.

There are different approaches that we can use to run or execute Jasmine test specs with PhantomJS. First, we can use any of the existing test runners for Jasmine and other testing frameworks, as documented by PhantomJS, from the following URL:

```
https://github.com/ariya/phantomjs/wiki/Headless-Testing
```

Second, we can run a Jasmine test using the PhantomJS API by loading the spec runner page using the `webpage` API, which we learned from the previous chapter. After opening the page, we can manipulate the Jasmine result page using DOM traversal, which we learned from the previous chapter. After that, we can redirect the content to any other channel; it can be the console screen, a logfile, or a continuous integration system.

Alternatively, we can use the PhantomJS `run-jasmine.js` code example that is included in the PhantomJS download package. We will use this approach rather than creating our own since we are going to review the code itself. This is almost the same as the second approach. This code can be found in the `examples` folder when we extract the contents of the PhantomJS package.

We are not going to change any of the code we wrote earlier; we will use the same set of JavaScript files, but instead of running the test within the browser, we will use PhantomJS. We will call `phantomjs`, specify that it needs to run the `run-jasmine.js` script from the `examples` folder, and pass the `SpecRunner.html` file that we modified earlier as the third parameter. We need to make sure we are running the script in the same folder of `SpecRunner.html`, or we will need to specify either the relative or absolute path along with it.

```
sources — bash — 120×14
$ ~/phantomjs/bin/phantomjs ~/phantomjs/examples/run-jasmine.js SpecRunner.html
'waitFor()' finished in 213ms.

Calculator
Passing 5 specs

$
```

The preceding screenshot shows that our test was executed and all specs have been passed. The Jasmine result is now different from the browser since the PhantomJS Jasmine runner only displays the summary of the test. If the test fails, the output will be as shown in the following screenshot:

```
sources — bash — 120×14
$ ~/phantomjs/bin/phantomjs ~/phantomjs/examples/run-jasmine.js SpecRunner.html
'waitFor()' finished in 222ms.

Calculator

1 test(s) FAILED:

Calculator should able to subtract positive numbers.
Expected 4 to equal 5.

$
```

PhantomJS `run-jasmine.js` only displays the summary and list of failed tests. What if we want to display the list of passed test specs just like the result page in the browser? We can do this since we know how to manipulate the page content and extract certain elements. To do this, we first need to get our copy of `run-jasmine.js` and save it as `run-jasmine2.js`, which is our modified version.

Before we start upgrading the `run-jasmine.js` script, we need to understand how Jasmine renders the list of passed items. Using our browser and by loading our `SpecRunner.html` file, we can investigate and view the HTML content.

```
▼ <body>
  ▼ <div id="HTMLReporter" class="jasmine_reporter">
    ► <div class="banner">…</div>
    ► <ul class="symbolSummary">…</ul>
    ► <div class="alert">…</div>
    ▼ <div class="results">
      ▼ <div class="summary">
        ▼ <div class="suite passed">
            <a class="description" href="?spec=Calculator">Calculator</a>
          ▼ <div class="specSummary passed">
              <a class="description" href="?spec=Calculator%20should%20able%20to%20add%20positive%20numbers."
              should able to add positive numbers.">should able to add positive numbers</a>
            </div>
          ► <div class="specSummary passed">…</div>
          ► <div class="specSummary passed">…</div>
          ► <div class="specSummary passed">…</div>
          ► <div class="specSummary passed">…</div>
          </div>
        </div>
        <div id="details"></div>
      </div>
```

The preceding screenshot displays code that contains the content of the generated HTML from Jasmine `SpecRunner.html` when tests have run. It shows us that there are several layers of `<div>` that are added for each spec with specific functional labels based on the CSS class. The result of the test is enclosed on a `<div>` tag with a CSS class attribute of `results`. Within `results`, there is a `summary` class attribute that contains the list of suites that were `passed`. Each suite has `description` and the list of items that were passed, as denoted by the CSS class `specSummary passed`.

All keywords that are mentioned in the code format in the previous paragraph are CSS class names that are available for us to use for traversing the Jasmine HTML result document.

We now have some understanding of what the Jasmine result HTML document's structure is. There can be more than one test suite, so we need to get all of the test suites that were executed.

```
var listPasssedSuites = document.body.querySelectorAll
  ('.results > .summary > .suite.passed');
if (listPasssedSuites && listPasssedSuites.length > 0) {
  for (i = 0; i < listPasssedSuites.length; ++i) {
    console.log(listPasssedSuites[i].
      querySelector('.description').innerText);

    var items = listPasssedSuites[i].querySelectorAll
      ('.specSummary.passed');
    for (j = 0; j < items.length; ++j) {
      console.log("     " +
        items[j].querySelector('.description').innerText);
    }
  }
}
```

Using the `querySelectorAll()` function in the preceding code, we can search and retrieve all of the elements having the same selector path from the document body. This function will give an array of elements for each test suite.

And from that list of test suites, we can search for all of the test items based on each element using the selector path of `'.specSummary.passed'`. The query will also return a list of elements having the test items' details. We can now traverse the content of the list to output for each test item's name, as shown in the preceding code.

Our previous enhancement can be inserted in `run-jasmine2.js`; it falls on the `else` block of the original code, where the code for displaying the number of passing items is located.

```
    return 1;
  } else {
    console.log(document.body.querySelector
      ('.alert > .passingAlert.bar').innerText);
    return 0;
  }
});
phantom.exit(exitCode);
```

After the insertion of the code, the following will be our new code:

```
    return 1;
  } else {
    var listPasssedSuites = document.body.querySelectorAll
      ('.results > .summary > .suite.passed');
    if (listPasssedSuites && listPasssedSuites.length > 0) {
      for (i = 0; i < listPasssedSuites.length; ++i) {
        console.log(listPasssedSuites[i].
          querySelector('.description').innerText);

        var items = listPasssedSuites[i].querySelectorAll
          ('.specSummary.passed');
        for (j = 0; j < items.length; ++j) {
          console.log("     " +
            items[j].querySelector('.description').innerText);
        }
      }
    }
    console.log(document.body.querySelector
      ('.alert > .passingAlert.bar').innerText);
    return 0;
  }
});
phantom.exit(exitCode);
```

When we run our new test runner and have had our entire test passed, we should have the following screenshot as the output:

```
○ ○ ○                    sources — bash — 120×14
$ ~/phantomjs/bin/phantomjs ~/phantomjs/examples/run-jasmine2.js SpecRunner.html
'waitFor()' finished in 219ms.

Calculator
Calculator
    should able to add positive numbers
    should able to add negative numbers
    should able to subtract positive numbers
    should able to subtract negative numbers
    should able to multiply numbers
Passing 5 specs
```

This is just an example of how we can customize our test runner to use it with Jasmine. Different development organizations have their own way and requirements for testing, and if we are engaging in doing testing for JavaScript and other web applications, this approach is very useful.

Summary

We can integrate PhantomJS and Jasmine test specs with other tools, such as continuous integration tools, that can execute these tests unattended. More organizations are adapting PhantomJS into their automated and headless testing for web applications. In some cases, people also use PhantomJS to perform stress and load testing for web applications.

11
Maximizing PhantomJS

Now that we have learned PhantomJS scripting and its features, let us go one step further and check out what other possibilities we have to maximize the capabilities of PhantomJS. We will look into integrating the third-party libraries with PhantomJS and also check out other tools that integrate with PhantomJS.

CasperJS

With the rising popularity of PhantomJS, there has been an evolution of several projects that integrate with or are based on PhantomJS. Some of these are extensions that enhance the scripting ability of PhantomJS.

CasperJS is an open source extension for PhantomJS. It extends the API of PhantomJS to make tasks such as web scraping, testing, and DOM manipulation easier. CasperJS can be downloaded from `http://casperjs.org`.

Let us see some basic PhantomJS and CasperJS code in action.

```
var casper = require("casper").create();
casper.start("http://www.phantomjs.org", function(){
  this.echo(this.getTitle());
});

casper.run();
```

If you look closely at the previous code, there is no trace of any PhantomJS API code having been used, except for the `require()` function.

CasperJS still uses PhantomJS and depends on the PhantomJS API; however, it provides its own unique API. CasperJS modules come with a new set of API functions. These functions introduce new features by wrapping up the PhantomJS API.

Then, we've used the CasperJS `start()` function, which is comparable to the PhantomJS `open()` function. If we are going to investigate CasperJS source code for the `start()` function, we find that it also calls the PhantomJS `open()` function.

However, the CasperJS coding style and approach is quite different from that of PhantomJS. CasperJS uses a step-by-step coding approach, which is also called **navigation scripting**. In the preceding code, we can see that this is applied as we define our first step in the second line; however, we only perform all of the defined steps when the CasperJS `run()` function is called. If we don't include the `run()` call in our code, there will be no execution of the code. Let us add more steps to our previous example.

```
var casper = require("casper").create();
casper.start("http://www.phantomjs.org", function(){
  this.echo(this.getTitle());
});

casper.then(function(){
  var version = this.evaluate(function(){
    return document.querySelector('.version').innerText;
  });
  this.echo(version);
});

casper.run();
```

In the preceding code, we've added a new step using the `then()` function of CasperJS. This function will accept a new function definition which will be added to the queue of steps. In this function definition, we attempt to get the current version of PhantomJS by using the DOM `querySelector()` function. Finally, we print out the version text to the console using CasperJS's `echo()` function, which is similar to `console.log()`.

Notice that we have a `start()` function followed by one or more `then()` functions, all started by the `run()` function. This represents the idiomatic way to write CasperJS scripts.

More than just an extension API, CasperJS can also be used to create test scripts that can be an alternative to Jasmine. It provides a very easy-to-use library that converts our script into a unit test. We'll modify our preceding script and insert some assertions:

```
var casper = require("casper").create();
casper.start("http://www.phantomjs.org", function(){
```

```
    this.echo(this.getTitle());
  });

  casper.then(function(){
    var version = this.evaluate(function(){
      return document.querySelector('.version').innerText;
    });
    casper.test.assertEquals(version, 'v1.9');
  });

  casper.run(function(){
    casper.test.done();
    casper.test.renderResults(true, 0);
  });
```

We've modified a few areas to make it a test script. In the preceding code snippet, we assert that the `version` string we scraped from the page equals to what we expect. Here, we use the `casper.test.assertEquals` function, which tests two objects for equality. We've also modified the `casper.run()` function and passed it with a closure, which will be called after all the steps are executed. This is the best location in our code to display the result of our tests because it runs at the very end. We call the `capser.test.done()` function to indicate that all the tests are executed and `casper.test.renderResults()` to display the summary of our tests. Running our new test script will give us the output shown in the following screenshot:

CasperJS is a nifty extension of PhantomJS, which can save us a lot of small and trivial code problems while writing scripts. It is also worth noting that developers are very prompt and visibly active in supporting and adapting new features of PhantomJS.

GhostDriver

GhostDriver is another component that was written to support Selenium's WebDriver Wire Protocol (`https://code.google.com/p/selenium/wiki/JsonWireProtocol`), and it is integrated with PhantomJS. Using GhostDriver, we can execute and play back Selenium test suites.

GhostDriver's syntax is straightforward and easy to use. There is no need of any other component since the feature is built into PhantomJS. To start a GhostDriver remote server, we use the following syntax:

```
phantomjs --webdriver=8080
          --webdriver-selenium-grid-hub=http://127.0.0.1:4444
```

Once started, we can use this remote server as a normal Selenium WebDriver client. More information about Selenium can be found at `http://docs.seleniumhq.org/`.

Screenshots, web metrics, and more

There are more components that are built on top of PhantomJS. Several of them are related to capturing and saving web page screenshots.

The `capturejs` command-line tool can capture screenshots. It also allows you to modify the page before saving the image. For more information and code syntax, check out the documentation at `https://github.com/superbrothers/capturejs`.

`ChromaNope` aims to capture screenshots that will help developers check their site for color blindness. `ChromaNope` generates different screenshots for each type of color blindness. It uses PhantomJS to capture and generate screenshots. Check out `ChromaNope` in action at `http://chromanope.com/`.

If you are interested in metrics, `confess.js` is something worth looking into. It will provide you with metrics, resources, timestamps, and other metadata. It will also create a waterfall-like graph of the resources, matching their request time and duration. `confess.js` can be downloaded from `https://github.com/jamesgpearce/confess`. These are just some of the components that are notable extensions of PhantomJS.

There are many projects and extensions being developed for and with PhantomJS, ranging from simple web services to screenshot capture, web testing extensions, and more. We can find out more about other PhantomJS-related tools at `https://github.com/ariya/phantomjs/wiki/Related-Projects`.

Summary

As we come to the end of this journey, let us embrace PhantomJS as more than just a headless browser or an extension to execute JavaScript. It also brings new dimensions and possibilities to our development, be it by actual product creation or supporting our web development through testing. It is not just a headless browser; as the Web has become more prevalent, the need for tools such as PhantomJS has expanded, and PhantomJS has certainly fulfilled the need.

Go beyond with PhantomJS and, hopefully, with our newfound knowledge, you will be inspired to create cool, new applications and extensions of this technology.

Index

G

getElementByClassName method 23
getElementById method 23
getElementByName method 23
getElementByTagName method 23
GhostDriver 120
Google 77
Google Direction API
  about 77
  URL 80

H

HTTP Archive (HAR) format 51

I

image formats
  GIF 69
  JPEG 69
  PNG 69
IP address based
  locations, checking 75-77
IP geolocation services
  about 75
  freegeoip.net 75
  hostip.info 75
  ipinfodb.com 75
it() function 105

J

Jasmine
  downloading 105
  URL 103, 104
  URL, for downloading 105
  used, for unit testing 104
Jasmine matchers
  URL 106
Jasmine Spec Runner 105
Jasmine test spec
  coding 105-111
  executing, with PhantomJS 111-115
JavaScript API, PhantomJS
  about 13
  FileSystem API 14

Module API 14
System API 14
WebPage API 14
WebServer API 15

K

keyboard events
  using 54-57

L

lib folder 105
location
  checking, based on IP address 75-77

M

MapQuest 77
Mocha 103
Module API 14
modules 95-97
mouse clicks
  simulating 30
mouse events
  using 57

N

navigation scripting 118

O

object-oriented modules
  using 98-100
onConfirm function 53
onError function 60
onLoadFinished event 41-43
onLoadStarted event 41-43
onResourceReceived event 45
onResourceRequested event handler 43
onUrlChanged function 51
opened files
  closing 87
open() function 85, 118

Thank you for buying
Getting Started with PhantomJS

About Packt Publishing

Packt, pronounced 'packed', published its first book "*Mastering phpMyAdmin for Effective MySQL Management*" in April 2004 and subsequently continued to specialize in publishing highly focused books on specific technologies and solutions.

Our books and publications share the experiences of your fellow IT professionals in adapting and customizing today's systems, applications, and frameworks. Our solution based books give you the knowledge and power to customize the software and technologies you're using to get the job done. Packt books are more specific and less general than the IT books you have seen in the past. Our unique business model allows us to bring you more focused information, giving you more of what you need to know, and less of what you don't.

Packt is a modern, yet unique publishing company, which focuses on producing quality, cutting-edge books for communities of developers, administrators, and newbies alike. For more information, please visit our website: www.packtpub.com.

About Packt Open Source

In 2010, Packt launched two new brands, Packt Open Source and Packt Enterprise, in order to continue its focus on specialization. This book is part of the Packt Open Source brand, home to books published on software built around Open Source licences, and offering information to anybody from advanced developers to budding web designers. The Open Source brand also runs Packt's Open Source Royalty Scheme, by which Packt gives a royalty to each Open Source project about whose software a book is sold.

Writing for Packt

We welcome all inquiries from people who are interested in authoring. Book proposals should be sent to author@packtpub.com. If your book idea is still at an early stage and you would like to discuss it first before writing a formal book proposal, contact us; one of our commissioning editors will get in touch with you.

We're not just looking for published authors; if you have strong technical skills but no writing experience, our experienced editors can help you develop a writing career, or simply get some additional reward for your expertise.

Backbone.js Testing

ISBN: 978-1-78216-524-8   Paperback: 168 pages

Plan, architect, and develop tests for Backbone.js applications using modern testing principles and practices

1. Create comprehensive test infrastructures

2. Understand and utilize modern frontend testing techniques and libraries

3. Use mocks, spies, and fakes to effortlessly test and observe complex Backbone.js application behavior

4. Automate tests to run from the command line, shell, or practically anywhere

Instant Node.js Starter

ISBN: 978-1-78216-556-9   Paperback: 48 pages

Program your scalable network applications and web services with Node.js

1. Learn something new in an Instant!
    A short, fast, focused guide delivering immediate results

2. Learn how to use module patterns and Node Packet Manager (NPM) in your applications

3. Discover callback patterns in NodeJS

4. Understand the use Node.js streams in your applications

Please check **www.PacktPub.com** for information on our titles

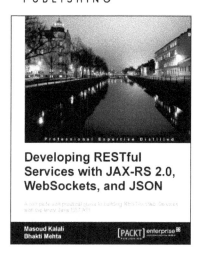

Developing RESTful
Services with JAX-RS 2.0,
WebSockets, and JSON

Masoud Kalali
Bhakti Mehta

[PACKT] enterprise

Developing RESTful Services with JAX-RS 2.0, WebSockets, and JSON

ISBN: 978-1-78217-812-5   Paperback: 128 pages

A complete and practical guide to building RESTful Web Services with the latest Java EE7 API

1. Learning about different client/server communication models including but not limited to client polling, Server-Sent Events and WebSockets

2. Efficiently use WebSockets, Server-Sent Events, and JSON in Java EE applications

3. Learn about JAX-RS 2.0 new features and enhancements

Getting Started with HTML5
WebSocket Programming

Develop and deploy your first secure and scalable
real-time web application

Vangos Pterneas   PACKT

Getting Started with HTML5 WebSocket Programming

ISBN: 978-1-78216-696-2   Paperback: 110 pages

Develop and deploy your first secure and scalable real-time web application

1. Start real-time communication in your web applications

2. Create a feature-rich WebSocket chat application

3. Learn the step-by-step configuration of the server and clients

Please check **www.PacktPub.com** for information on our titles

www.ingramcontent.com/pod-product-compliance
Lightning Source LLC
Chambersburg PA
CBHW060150060326
40690CB00018B/4050